Madonna

The Illustrated Biography

Madonna

The Illustrated Biography

MARIE CLAYTON

This edition published by
Welcome Rain Publishers LLC in 2010

First published by Transatlantic Press in 2010

Transatlantic Press
38 Copthorne Road
Croxley Green
Hertfordshire
WD3 4AQ

© Transatlantic Press
All images © Getty Images

978-1-56649-098-6

Printed and bound in China

Contents

Introduction

Born in Bay City, Michigan, on August 16, 1958, Madonna Louise Veronica was the third child of Madonna and Silvio Ciccone. When she was only five years old her mother died and Madonna said later that her loss so early was a major factor in her attitude to life: "I think the biggest reason I was able to express myself and not be intimidated was by not having a mother. For example, mothers teach you manners. And I absolutely did not learn any of those rules and regulations." At High School she was a straight-A student – but is also remembered for her provocative behavior. A talented dancer, she won a scholarship to study dance at the University of Michigan, but by 1977 had moved to New York to become a professional dancer. There she became involved in the music scene and soon reinvented herself as a rock star, with the songs she produced quickly leading to a recording contract with Sire Records—and a string of hit singles. Able to blend song with dance to create a mesmerizing performance—Madonna was soon entertaining and shocking in equal measure.

In 1985 the rising star married brat-pack actor Sean Penn but their stormy relationship was constantly in the news and they soon divorced. Her work began to include material that led to a negative response from some parts of the establishment and her audience. However, Madonna was soon able to reinvent herself again and in 1996 she starred in the movie *Evita*, gaining critical recognition for her role, while her next album was acclaimed for its lyrical depth. The birth of her daughter, Lourdes, in 1996, coincided with Madonna discovering Eastern mysticism and the Kabbalah religion, which she credited with her change to a new, softer self. In 1999 she met British film director Guy Ritchie and they married and had a son, Rocco. Madonna moved to Britain and began a new life that combined country pursuits, such as horse-riding, with a continuing career as one of the most iconic female singers of a generation.

Madonna's spectacular concert tours are legendary and are some of the highest-grossing events of their kind. Most of her records have been hits and she is certified as the best-selling female rock artist of the 20th century. Today she is known as one of the most influential women in music, with a talent for reinvention that always keeps her career fresh and on track.

Part One

Material Girl

1982: First appearance of a star

Opposite and left: Publicity photographs of Madonna taken around the time her first album, *Madonna* was released in July 1983. She had initially come to New York in 1977 to become a professional dancer and worked with several modern dance troupes—although often had to supplement her income with odd jobs. She later joined a rock band, Breakfast Club, and formed several bands of her own, including Emmy, with musician and former boyfriend Stephen Bray.

The songs Madonna produced with Bray caught the attention of DJ and record producer Mark Kamins and he took her to meet Seymour Stein, founder of Sire Records, a label owned at that time by Warner Bros. Records. Her first record, "Everybody" was released on April 24, 1982 and was at first promoted to black audiences; it didn't feature a picture of Madonna, which gave rise to the misconception that she was African-American. Later she persuaded Sire to produce a music video of her performing the song, which brought her attention and caused the song to move up the dance charts.

Setting a new style

Above: Madonna had a very distinctive look and was a visually stunning performer even in the very early days of her career. Her style was created with the help of artist and fashion designer Maripol, and was based around multiple bracelets—often of rubber—crucifixes, lace tops, and skirts over capri pants. The look soon began to influence other young women and became a popular fashion trend during the 1980s.

Opposite: Madonna with singer Marilyn, backstage at a nightclub in New York in 1983. At this time Madonna was working on material for her forthcoming debut album, *Madonna*, which went on to sell more than 3 million copies. At the end of 1982 and into the beginning of 1983 she was romantically involved with artist Jean-Michel Basquiat, even living with him for a short time, but the artist's escalating drug use and late hours soon took their toll and in early 1983 they split up.

Like A Virgin

Opposite: A posed publicity shot released in 1984. The first album had been a slow but steady success, so Madonna was now working on the follow-up album, *Like A Virgin*, which was released in November 1984. The new album hit No. 1 on the *Billboard* 200 chart and went platinum within a month. The title single was her first No. 1 chart success, hitting the top spot in the *Billboard* Hot 100 and staying there for six weeks. She sang "Like a Virgin" at the first MTV Video Music Awards in September 1984, writhing suggestively around the stage in a wedding dress. Her performance was judged to be outrageous by some, but later came to be widely regarded as one of the iconic moments in the history of pop music.

Right: On stage during a concert at Madison Square Garden in New York in 1984. Madonna had developed her love of singing combined with dance during a stint in a show in Paris towards the end of the 1970s. It was the song "Holiday"—from the first album but which was also released as a single towards the end of 1983—that earned the singer one of her first appearances on television, on *Dick Clark's American Bandstand* in 1984. In her interview during the show, she told Clark that her main ambition was "to rule the world."

Desperately Seeking Susan

Above: Madonna and actress Rosanna Arquette filmed *Desperately Seeking Susan* in 1984, and it was released the following year. Although Rosanna Arquette was the star and Madonna only had a small role, the movie became widely regarded as a Madonna "vehicle"—and despite her star status Rosanna won a BAFTA Award for Best Actress in a Supporting Role. Madonna also performed the soundtrack's single, "Into the Groove," which soon reached No. 1 on the U.S. dance charts.

Opposite: With John "Jellybean" Benitez at the opening of the video club Private Eyes in July 1984. Jellybean, a musician and music producer, had become Madonna's new romantic partner after they were introduced by Stephen Bray. Madonna's 8th single "Crazy for You," which she had performed when appearing as a bar room singer in the 1985 film *Vision Quest*, also became an instant No. 1 hit.

An award nomination

Left and opposite: At the 12th Annual American Music Awards in January 1985. Madonna had been nominated for Favorite Pop/Rock Female Artist, but lost out to Cyndi Lauper. She is seen left with Huey Lewis, who had been nominated in a different category with his band The News. That January Madonna also shot a music video for her latest single "Material Girl" in Hollywood and it was during the shoot that she first saw brat-pack actor Sean Penn. She later said that she was about to descend a red-carpeted staircase for one of the video's scenes, when she looked down and saw Penn, invited to the shoot by its director, his friend Mary Lambert. She was immediately attracted to him, and the two of them began dating soon afterwards. The world's press found their relationship fascinating: pop's newest young star dating the angry, hard-drinking, artistically-driven Penn and it was not long before photographers were constantly hounding the couple.

The "Virgin" tour

Opposite and right: Madonna on stage at St. Paul, Minnesota, during her first tour around North America, which was dubbed the Virgin tour. It began in Seattle in April 1985 and finished on June 11 in New York City, visiting most major U.S. cities as well as Toronto in Canada. The venues initially booked had been small, but demand for tickets was so high that shows had to be re-scheduled to larger auditoriums. More dates were also added in some cities – all the tickets for Madonna's show at New York City's prestigious Radio City Music Hall were completely sold out in a record-breaking 34 minutes, and a similar demand for tickets was reported from many other venues. Initial press reviews were not that complimentary about her singing abilities, but noted that the fans went wild as soon as she appeared on stage and carried on screaming throughout most of the performance. This first tour was a relatively simple pop concert—later tours became much more spectacular. Some of her stage outfits were revealing and she teased the audience with sexual innuendo as she sang—she already knew how to entertain and shock at the same time.

July 1985: Live Aid

Opposite and right: Onstage on July 13 during Live Aid, one of the most ambitious satellite link-ups and television broadcasts of all time and watched by an estimated 400 million viewers across 60 countries. Madonna appeared at the JFK Stadium venue in Philadelphia, introduced by actress Bette Midler as "a woman who has pulled herself up by her bra straps" and announced "I'm not taking off nothing today" in response to the furore surrounding the publication of nude photographs of her. She sang "Holiday," "Into the Groove," and "Love Makes the World Go Round." In Britain, "Into The Groove" was about to become the singer's first U.K. chart topper.

In September 1985 both *Penthouse* and *Playboy* published nude pictures of the new star from when she was a struggling young dancer in New York in 1979. They had been taken by famous photographer Lee Friedlander after Madonna had responded to his advertisement seeking a model. She had signed all the proper release forms at the time, so could do nothing to stop them being published—but anyway publicly she was unashamed and defiant. Ironically she had been paid only $25 at the time, but some of the photographs later changed hands for many thousands of dollars.

A couple in the spotlight

Left and opposite: Madonna and Sean Penn in July 1986 during rehearsals for *Goose and Tomtom* in New York—Madonna's first theater role, which Penn also starred in. The two had married on her birthday, August 16, 1985, but the ceremony was an indication of the stormy events to come. Penn wanted an open-air ceremony and had chosen the Malibu home of friend Kurt Unger, but their vows were almost drowned out by the sound of several media helicopters hovering overhead. Penn became so angry at the invasion of their privacy that once the ceremony was over he fetched a gun and started shooting into the sky. By contrast, Madonna had wanted an official photocall posing in her strapless white wedding gown—she was comfortable with the media attention and couldn't understand why Penn was so angry about it. It was the first of many arguments the two would have over appearing in public.

Shanghai Surprise

Above: The newly-weds were soon working together, filming the movie *Shanghai Surprise* on location in Hong Kong and London. Set in the 1930s, Penn played a fortune hunter hired by a pair of missionaries—one of whom was played by Madonna—to find a legendary source of opium that was needed to ease the pain of wounded soldiers. The press interest in the two was still unabated and Penn could not bear the constant harassment. In addition the two stars argued with each other and with the director over how the movie was to be made. Rumors of

run-ins with journalists and photographers soon began coming from the set and producer George Harrison quickly called a press conference to try to calm things down. Some reviews for both stars' performances and for the movie itself were vicious—although in fact it was both well made and entertaining.

Opposite: Madonna and Sean Penn pictured in August 1986.

Papa Don't Preach

Left and opposite: Shooting for the video to accompany "Papa Don't Preach" in May 1986. The video unveiled a new look—cropped blond hair instead of long, tousled locks, and a more muscular body. The record became Madonna's 4th No. 1 in the *Billboard* Hot 100 and also hit the top spot in the U.K., Australia, and many countries in Europe. The lyrics tell the story of a teenage girl who becomes pregnant, but refuses to have an abortion—as urged by her friends—or give up the baby for adoption, as suggested by her father. As such it immediately caused controversy – women's organizations said it encouraged teenage pregnancy, parenting organizations thought it undermined efforts to promote birth control, pro-lifers said it condemned abortion. Madonna herself said in an interview in *The New York Times*, "This song is really about a girl who is making a decision in her life. She has a very close relationship with her father and wants to maintain that closeness. To me it's a celebration of life. It says, 'I love you, Father, and I love this man and this child that is growing inside me.' Of course, who knows how it will end? But at least it starts off positive."

Visionary videos

Opposite: Madonna at the 2nd Annual Commitment to Life AIDS benefit in Los Angeles in September 1986. She had recently released her third album, *True Blue*, which included a song "Live to Tell" that was written for the movie *At Close Range* starring her husband Sean Penn. *Rolling Stone* praised the album, saying "It sounds as if it comes from the heart." It went on to become an international success, reaching the top of the charts in several countries and clocking up worldwide sales of more than 24 million copies.

Right: At the MTV Video Music Awards, aired live on September 5 from various locations, Madonna was honored with the Video Vanguard Award in recognition of her visionary music videos. "Papa Don't Preach" had recently been knocked from its No. 1 spot in the U.S. charts, but was still going strong across Europe and in Australia and went on to become one of the definitive songs in Madonna's career.

Favorite Female Video Artist

Left and opposite: At the 14th Annual American
Music Awards held on January 26, 1987,
Madonna won the Favorite Pop/Rock Female
Video Artist category and her single "Live To
Tell" was also nominated for Favorite Pop/Rock
Single. Madonna made a surprise appearance at
the Shrine Auditorium in Los Angeles to collect
her award. "Papa Don't Preach" had also
recently been honored as America's Most
Popular Video and World's Favorite Video at the
1st annual World Music Video Awards, produced
by Canada's MuchMusic and Europe's Sky
Channel. Madonna's career was riding high, as
the following month her most recent album,
True Blue, was certified platinum, her new single
"Open Your Heart" hit the No. 1 spot in the U.S.
and *Rolling Stone* magazine readers' poll voted
her Best Female Singer and Sexiest Female
Artist. Unfortunately, as her career rocketed her
into superstardom, that of her husband Sean
Penn had temporarily stalled and he was not
taking it well. He had been arrested and given
one year's probation for punching a man who
tried to kiss Madonna in a nightclub, but in
April 1987 he violated that probation when he
hit an extra on the set of *Colors* for trying to take
his photograph without permission.

Who's That Girl

Opposite and left: On stage during the Who's That Girl tour, which began in Osaka, Japan, on June 14 and covered eighteen cities on two continents, finishing on September 6 in Florence, Italy. In Japan, a thousand troops had to be deployed to restrain 25,000 fans waiting to greet Madonna at the airport and 144,000 tickets were sold for two shows at Wembley Stadium in London in just 18 hours. However, Madonna's personal life was not going well: in July she was taken to hospital for an X-ray after her husband apparently hit her Despite the injury she did not make an official complaint, because Penn was already about to serve the short jail term he had received for attacking the film extra on *Colors*. The violent arguments between them were draining for both, but Madonna could not bring herself to admit that the marriage had failed.

Taking Paris by storm

Left and opposite: On stage in front of 130,000 people at Parc de Sceaux, Paris, France—the highest attendance at a concert in France—at the end of July 1987 during the Who's That Girl tour. That May she had become the only female solo artist to have four No. 1 singles in U.K. when "La Isla Bonita" hit the top spot—and this quickly became five when "Who's That Girl" reached No. 1 in June. In the U.S. she was doing just as well: "Who's That Girl" was her sixth No. 1.

The Guinness Book Of Records in 1988 honored Madonna as the most successful singer for selling over 11 million copies of True Blue, which hit No. 1 in 28 countries and established her as the world's highest-selling solo singing artist.

A glittering premiere

Opposite: In August the movie *Who's That Girl* was released—Madonna is seen here arriving at the New York première in Times Square. She had begun filming it the previous November and it was to have been called *Slammer*, until she wrote the title song. Madonna played a feisty and free-spirited female ex-convict who asks an uptight New York tax lawyer, played by Griffin Dunne, to help prove her innocence. The movie did not do that well initially at the box office, but later came to be regarded as an offbeat hit in many countries.

Right: At a reception at Paris City Hall to meet French prime minister Jacques Chirac and his family, Madonna presents him with a check for $85,000 to benefit AIDS charities in France. In September she performed "Causing A Commotion" live via satellite from Turin, Italy and won Best Female Video for "Papa Don't Preach" at the 4th annual MTV Video Music Awards. But her marriage was still on a downward spiral and at the beginning of December, she filed divorce papers—although within less than two weeks she had withdrawn them.

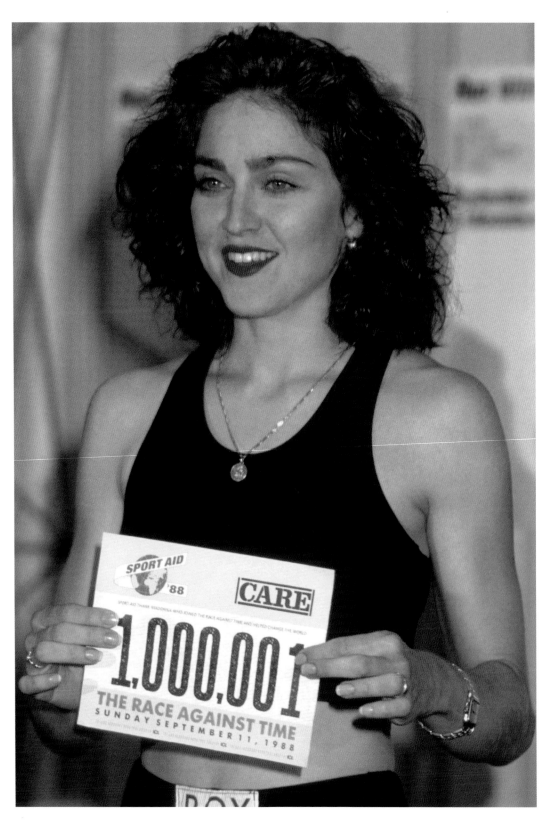

An ongoing passion for keeping fit

Left: Madonna participates in Sport Aid '88: The Race Against Time marathon in New York, N.Y., which was staged to help raise funds to fight the diseases that claimed the lives of millions of children each year. She had already begun her commitment to regular exercise, with one- to two-hour workout routines six times a week. Her trainer later said that the key to Madonna's ultra-fit physical shape was to constantly change the routine and mix dancing with other types of cardio training—such as treadmill sprints, jumping rope or running on a trampoline—as well as various other types of crunches and weight lifting. The constant switching prevented any group of muscles from bulking up.

Opposite: Jogging with her personal trainer and bodyguards while on tour in London. Even today she follows a punishing fitness regime: in April 2008 she told *Elle* magazine, "There are no short cuts to being Madonna, it's all about hard work. There is no easy way. If you want to know how I look like I do, it's diet and exercise and constantly being careful … I'm not going to slow down, get off this ride, stay home, and get fat!"

End of a marriage

Above: Madonna and Penn in 1987. In January 1989 Madonna filed for divorce again after a reported violent quarrel. She moved into a new house but in the end she dropped all assault charges and later said: "May God bless and keep him—but far, far from me. This marriage is over."

Opposite: Arriving at the première of *Speed-The-Plow*, Madonna's first appearance on the Broadway stage. Very soon after her marriage came to an end Madonna released one of her finest and most controversial singles, "Like A Prayer," while Penn began to appear in a succession of fine movies that quickly restored his artistic reputation.

Express Yourself

Left and opposite: Madonna performs "Express Yourself" at the 6th annual MTV Video Music Awards at the Universal Amphitheater, Los Angeles, California, in September 1989. "Express Yourself" won Best Direction, Best Art Direction, Best Cinematography and "Like A Prayer" won the Viewers' Choice Award. At the beginning of 1989 Madonna had signed a $5 million contract with Pepsi-Cola for a series of TV commercials and sponsorship of a world tour. The debut of the "Like a Prayer" video was on MTV in March, but it featured the suggestion of an interracial relationship, burning crosses, and a blend of sexual innuendo and religious symbols—and Pope John Paul II had soon urged fans not to attend Madonna concerts. Since the video was almost identical to the commercials Madonna had filmed as part of her contract with Pepsi, they quickly pulled out of their endorsement of the star.

Feeling Breathless

Left and opposite: Madonna out and about with actor Warren Beatty. In 1989 Madonna had begun filming *Dick Tracy*, based on the comic-book hero, which starred and was directed by Warren Beatty. She co-starred as Breathless Mahoney, a nightclub entertainer with a secret life. While working together she and Beatty began a romantic relationship and they were soon seen out and about together, but this came to a end late in 1990. Just before the release of the film in June 1990, the soundtrack album *I'm Breathless* was also released; it included songs that had been inspired by the 1930s era of the movie as well as her new single, which went on to become her 8th No. 1 in the *Billboard* charts. Meanwhile her previous album, *Like A Prayer*, had been certified platinum and had been named The Grand Prix Album Of The Year at the 4th annual Japan Gold Disc Awards in Tokyo.

Madonna had also recently had a small part as showgirl-with-a-heart-of-gold Hortense Hathaway in *The Bloodhounds of Broadway*, a comedy musical movie based on four short stories by Damon Runyon. The movie had been released in 1989, but in 1990 it came out on video and was also premièred on television under the *American Playhouse* format.

Blond Ambition tour

Opposite and right: On stage during the Blond Ambition tour, which began on April 13 in Tokyo, Japan, and finished on August 5 in Nice in the South of France. This was the first mega tour of the 1990s, covering 27 cities over nearly four months. It sold out in every city—except in Italy, where for weeks Pope John Paul II had called for a boycott, resulting in the cancelation of one of the two shows planned. Although Pepsi had pulled out, a new sponsor, Pioneer Electronics, had soon stepped in. Much of the tour was filmed for a movie to be released in May the following year. *Rolling Stone* magazine described Blond Ambition as an "elaborately choreographed, sexually provocative extravaganza" and proclaimed it "the best tour of 1990."

Not so much a show as a theatrical presentation...

Opposite and right: Talking about Blond Ambition, Madonna said, "My show is not a conventional rock show, but a theatrical presentation of my music. And like theater, it asks questions, provokes thoughts and takes you on an emotional journey, portraying good and bad, light and dark, joy and sorrow, redemption and salvation. I do not endorse a way of life, but describe one, and the audience is left to make its own decisions and judgments. This is what I consider freedom of speech, freedom of expression, and freedom of thought. Every night, before I go on stage, I say a prayer, not only that my show will go well, but that the audience will watch it with an open heart and an open mind, and see it as a celebration of love, life, and humanity." After the tour finished she said she would never go on tour again—but within three years she was off again with The Girlie Show.

The iconic costume with its cone brassiere was designed by French fashion designer Jean-Paul Gaultier. For the Japan and North American shows Madonna wore a blond ponytail hairpiece, as shown left, but it kept getting caught in her microphone and was pulling her real hair out, so on the European leg of the tour she had a mop of short blonde curls instead.

A stunning performance at the MTV Video Music Awards

Left: Madonna gave a stunning performance of her latest hit single "Vogue" at the 1990 MTV Video Music Awards. She and her dancers were dressed in 18th-century costumes – Madonna rather resembled the doomed French queen, Marie Antoinette. During her performance, she lifted her dress to flash her stocking tops and lacy underwear at the audience and later cradled the faces of two male dancers in her cleavage. The recording of this performance was later released as a music video; the original video for the song recalled the look of 1930s Hollywood films and had scenes based on portraits of Marilyn Monroe, Veronica Lake, and Marlene Dietrich. In some scenes Madonna's breasts could be seen through a sheer lace shirt, but she refused to cut these shots—although in some countries they were cut when the video was shown. At the time, "Vogue" was Madonna's highest-selling single worldwide, hitting the top spot in over thirty countries and selling over 6 million copies. It was the first to be certified as multi-platinum in the U.S.

A new romance

Left: Tony Ward had replaced Warren Beatty in Madonna's life towards the end of 1990 and she continued to date him for nearly a year. At the same time she was also seeing rapper Vanilla Ice. As a model, Ward was famous for a series of Calvin Klein adverts, which were photographed by Herb Ritts. He also worked with other major photographers and for well-known fashion brands. After he became involved with Madonna, he appeared in some of her music videos, notably that for "Justify My Love," which was banned from MTV but sold more than 250,000 copies as a "video single." In January 1991 Madonna had a small part in *Shadows And Fog*, starring John Malkovich and Mia Farrow, directed by Woody Allen.

Opposite: With Michael Jackson at the Oscars in March 1991. Madonna grabbed much of the attention in a low-cut, pearl-encrusted Bob Mackie gown, with $20 million in diamonds, on loan from jeweler Harry Winston, but Michael was certainly not outdone in his gold-tipped cowboy boots, a sequin and pearl encrusted jacket, and a massive diamond brooch. After Michael died Madonna paid a moving tribute to him at the 2009 MTV Video Music Awards, remembering her brief friendship with him in the early 1990s, and commenting that he seemed vulnerable and human to her then and as if he had needed a friend.

Truth or Dare

Opposite and right: The New York première of *Truth or Dare* —known as *In Bed With Madonna* outside North America—a two-hour combination of footage taken during the Blond Ambition tour and raunchy offstage scenes. It so shocked the Motion Picture Association of America that they dubbed even the trailer too racy for G-or PG-rated audiences. Among the outrageous scenes, Madonna demonstrated sex techniques; recited an ode to flatulence; ogled two male dancers as they French-kissed; exposed her breasts; and confessed that, as a teenager, she had sex with a girlfriend. However, apart from these deliberate attempts to shock, the film also has many unexpectedly human moments that are probably a major reason why it was so well-received. Most critics loved it and it was very successful, earning more than $29 million at the box office and becoming one of the highest-grossing documentaries ever.

It was not only Madonna's movies that were breaking records: in March 1991, her new single "Rescue Me" had become the highest debuting single in chart history to date when it entered the *Billboard* Hot 100 at No. 15, beating the previous record set by Michael Jackson's "Thriller."

Taking Cannes by storm...

Opposite: Madonna at the Cannes film festival in May 1991, where her film, *Truth or Dare*, was being shown outside competition. The night before the screening, Dino DeLaurentis, who was distributing the film, threw a party for Madonna that quickly became the hottest event of the festival. In the film, the onstage sequences were shot in color, but the remainder is in black and white. During one scene the star is asked who has been the love of her life for her whole life, her biggest love, and without hesitation she says, "Sean."

Above: With Tony Ward at a benefit dinner in May 1991. The following July she began filming *A League Of Their Own*, starring Tom Hanks and Geena Davis, directed by Penny Marshall. The movie was based on the founding of the women's professional baseball league in America in the 1940s, and Madonna was one of the players, Mae "All The Way" Mordabito. Released in July the following year, the movie was a commercial success and soon went to No. 1.

Revealing all on the catwalk

Opposite: Madonna with French fashion designer Jean-Paul Gaultier on a catwalk in Los Angeles, modeling one of his outfits that exposes her breasts. The show was a benefit and raised $750,000 for the American Foundation For AIDS Research. Gaultier was well known for his sexy, irreverent clothing and had designed many of Madonna's outfits for her Blond Ambition tour.

   In April 1992 Madonna had formed her own entertainment company, Maverick, to cover film production, record production, music and book publishing, as well as television and merchandising.

Right: At a pre-publication party on October 15 to launch Madonna's *Sex*, an erotic coffee-table book that featured the star in a variety of erotic poses. Despite its content, *Sex* was the most successful coffee table book ever published. It sold 150,000 copies on publication day in the U.S. alone and within three days all 1.5 million copies of the first worldwide edition had sold out. The album *Erotica* was released at the same time and by the end of 1993 had reached double platinum status. A review in *Rolling Stone* magazine said, "*Erotica* is everything Madonna has been denounced for being—meticulous, calculated, domineering, and artificial. It accepts those charges and answers with a brilliant record to prove them."

Body of Evidence

Opposite: Madonna leaving her apartment in New York in 1993. Her latest movie *Body Of Evidence*, in which she co-starred with Willem Dafoe, had been released on January 15 and grossed $6.5 million at the U.S. box office on its opening weekend. The steamy plot had Madonna on trial for murdering her much older millionaire lover with a bout of kinky sex, in order to inherit his money. Her lawyer, played by Dafoe, quickly succumbs to her charms but soon begins to wonder if he's defending a murderess. The graphic sex scenes had to be censored even to achieve an R-rating, but they were restored for the later video release. Madonna herself was nominated for an MTV Movie Award as Most Desirable Female, but otherwise the film did not enjoy wide critical acclaim.

Above: Enjoying the NBA game between the Chicago Bulls and the New York Knickerbockers on June 4, 1993. In February she had started filming *Dangerous Game*, co-starring Harvey Kietel and James Russo, and directed by Abel Ferrerra. It was premièred at the 50th annual Venice Film Festival in Venice, Italy, but Madonna was apparently not happy with the plot and was quoted as saying, "Even though it's a shit movie and I hate it, I am good in it." Her comments enraged the director, who felt they had been a big factor in its subsequent box office failure. Ironically, it was one of the few films for which Madonna received good reviews from the critics. She also released three new singles in 1993: "Bad Girl" in February, "Fever" in March, and "Rain" in July, plus "Bye Bye Baby" in Japan.

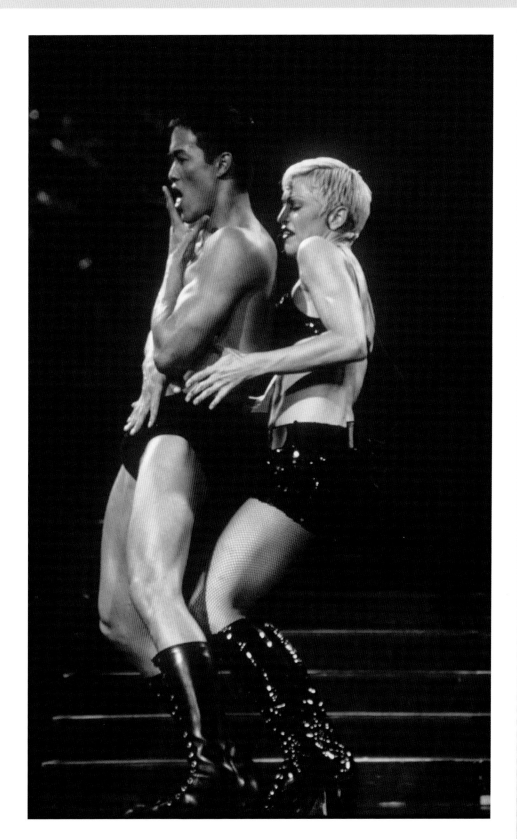

The Girlie Show tour

Opposite and right: On stage singing "Fever" during
The Girlie Show world tour, which started on
September 25 in London. It covered the United
Kingdom, France, Israel, Turkey, North America,
Puerto Rico, Argentina, Brazil, Australia, and Japan
and finished on December 19 in Tokyo. The show was
based around the album *Erotica*, so many of the main
visual set pieces had sexual overtones. One section of
the show featured a topless dancer – who had to
cover up at some venues to avoid breaking anti-nudity
laws. Unusually there were only five dates in the
U.S.—*Erotica* had not done that well in America and
there had been a big negative backlash after the
publication of *Sex*. In Israel—where Madonna was
performing for the first time—Orthodox Jews tried to
stop the show with demonstrations and rallies. The
different sections of the show meant 1500 costumes
were needed for the cast, which were all designed by
Dolce and Gabbana. The enormous and complex
stage took 24 hours to set up, with its revolving
elevated platform and balconies at the rear, as well as
a runway that led from the center of the main stage to
a minor stage. The core of the show took place in a
disco stage setting with glittering Mylar curtains and
mirrored balls.

In September, *Rolling Stone* magazine published its
list of 100 Top Music Videos and Madonna had more
videos in the list than any other artist: "Express
Yourself" at No. 10, "Like A Prayer" at No. 20,
"Borderline" at No. 24, "Vogue" at No. 28, "Justify My
Love" at No. 43 and "Oh Father" at No. 66.

A great entertainer

Opposite: Madonna performs "Vogue" during The Girlie Show. The name of the tour was inspired by a 1941 painting called "Girlie Show" by Edward Hopper, which shows a burlesque dancer. Burlesque was a theme that ran though many of the set pieces in the show and another source of inspiration was Gene Kelly: complete segments from Kelly's 1952 legendary musical *Singin' In The Rain* were used during the "Rain" section. A review in The New York Times said: "... after the proudly uningratiating Blond Ambition tour in 1990, not to mention the *Sex* book last year, 'The Girlie Show' tweaks fewer taboos. Despite the naughty bits, most of the two-hour show is devoted to repositioning Madonna from trend-spotter to part-time nostalgia merchant, and from titillating novelty act to all-around entertainer ... in The Girlie Show, which started its three-night stand at Madison Square Garden on Thursday, she's likable again." Some critics lamented the fact that the show's omission of Madonna's established hits, but most fans enjoyed seeing her perform new material.

Right: The blond afro wig that Madonna wore for some sections was inspired by the 1932 film *Blonde Venus*, starring Marlene Dietrich. The various sections of the show were linked by the appearance of a clown, who at the end appears again and is revealed to be Madonna herself. A photo book that documented the show, *The Girlie Show*, was published the following August.

Part Two

You Must
Love Me

1994: A change of image

Opposite: At the première of *With Honors* in Los Angeles. Madonna sang the theme song for the movie, "I'll Remember," which quickly went to No. 2 in the U.S. charts and within three months had been certified gold after selling 500,000 copies. The song marked a departure in style—it was a tender ballad and in the music video Madonna sports cropped black hair and an androgynous look.

Above: With Rosie Perez at the 8th Annual Soul Train Awards on March 15 in Los Angeles. Although Madonna had toned down her image a little, at the end of the month she caused public outrage again when she appeared on CBS-TV's *Late Show With David Letterman* and used several swear words as well as telling lewd jokes and being rude to her host. However, Letterman had introduced her by saying she had slept with most of the big names in the entertainment industry.

Making a change

Opposite: With Alek Keshishian, director of *With Honors*. A negative backlash had been building up from both the media and her fans since the release of *Sex*, the album *Erotica* and *Body of Evidence*—all of which featured explicit sexual imagery and had come out around the same time—with many feeling that she had now gone too far and that her career was over. Madonna had begun to realize that her provocative

behavior had certainly brought her attention, but had alienated many ordinary fans as well as the press. To sustain her career in the long term she would need to reinvent herself and she soon set about the process.

Above: On stage at the 1995 MTV Video Music Awards in New York City.

Take a bow

Opposite: A still from the music video for "Take a Bow," which was directed by Michael Haussman. It was filmed in Spain in period style, with Madonna playing the lover of a bullfighter. At the time she was being considered for the role of Eva Peron in the forthcoming movie of the musical *Evita*. The ballad "Take a Bow" was released in December and quickly went to No. 1 in the U.S. charts, the first time Madonna had managed to hit the top spot again after a gap of nearly three years. It stayed at No. 1 for seven weeks, which was the longest run in this position the singer had achieved so far, and went on to become the highest-selling single of 1995.

Above: At the 11th annual MTV Video Music Awards held in New York City in September. Madonna, along with David Letterman, presented the Video of the Year award to Aerosmith for "Cryin." In her personal life, Madonna had been spending some time in court. August had seen the trial of stalker Todd Lawrence, who received a one-year jail sentence, while earlier in September she had reached an out-of-court settlement with three dancers from the Blond Ambition tour. In 1992 they had filed a lawsuit against her, claiming that having their private lives exposed in *Truth or Dare*, the movie of the tour, had been an invasion of privacy and had caused emotional distress.

A new man

Left: In September 1994, Madonna met Carlos Leon, a New Yorker of Cuban descent, who soon became her personal trainer. The two of them also quickly became romantically involved and were seen out and about together. Leon had reportedly seen Madonna jogging in Central Park, where he also ran every day, and decided to approach her. He said later that Madonna took her fitness regime so seriously that she was better than most trainers. He himself had taken to exercise after noticing how unhealthy many of his Cuban relatives seemed to be and it had then developed into a career.

Opposite: With Kenny "Babyface" Edmonds at the 22nd annual American Music Awards in January 1995. The R&B singer had co-written, co-produced and provided backing vocals on her song "Take a Bow."

Madonna throws a Pajama Party

Opposite: Madonna sings "Bedtime Story" at the 1995 BRIT Awards— the first time she had performed at them—at Alexandra Palace in London in February. The song had been written for her by Icelandic singer Björk, and had only just been released in the U.S.—it was not due to come out in the U.K. until the following month. It reached the top five in charts in the U.K. and Australia, and became No. 1 in the U.S. dance club hit list, but only made it to No. 42 in the *Billboard* Hot 100 chart. It was the third single from the 1994 album, *Bedtime Stories*—the others were "Secret" and "Take a Bow."

Right: On March 18, 1995, MTV broadcast live from Madonna's Bedtime Story Pajama Party, an exclusive invitation-only event held at New York City's Webster Hall. Radio station Z-100 had held a contest to choose the 1500 lucky fans to attend, all of whom had to come in nightwear. Madonna and Jr. Vazquez acted as DJs for the event, which was also aired live on Z-100. Only a few days earlier it had been confirmed that Madonna had been signed to play Eva Peron in the forthcoming movie of *Evita*.

Meet the Champ

Opposite: Madonna with Muhammad Ali at the Parkinson's Disease Foundation salute to the former Heavyweight Champion at the Marriott Marquis Hotel in New York City on June 1. In her speech introducing Ali, Madonna said, "We're very much alike in many ways. We have espoused unpopular causes. We are arrogant. We like to have our picture taken, and we are the greatest."

The previous day, a security guard at Madonna's Castillo del Lago estate in Los Angeles had shot Robert Hoskins, a fan who had managed to gain access to the grounds of the estate several times by scaling the wall. During a previous incident Hoskins had told the guard that if Madonna did not marry him that very evening, he would slice her throat open. On that occasion he was forced to leave the grounds and the police were called, but they were unable to find Hoskins to arrest him. This time Hoskins was arrested and was sentenced to 10 years in Jail. At his trial in January 1996, Madonna was called to testify about the trauma Hoskins had caused her, and said that she had repeated nightmares of him actually getting into her home and finding her. However, in the view of California Deputy District Attorney Rhonda Saunders, the press made a comedy out of her ordeal, which undermined efforts to bring attention to the real dangers involved in such cases.

Right: Madonna spotted in New York City with her dog, Chiquita.

Taking a bow...

Left and opposite: At the 12th MTV Video
Music Awards with Anthony Kiedis, lead singer
of the Red Hot Chili Peppers. The awards were
broadcast live from Radio City Music Hall in
New York City on September 7, 1995. Madonna
won Best Female Video for "Take a Bow" and
also presented the Best Rap Video award to Dr.
Dre for "Keep Their Heads Ringin'."

Later that month she was due to leave the
U.S. for England, where she was to begin
recording the soundtrack for her forthcoming
movie, *Evita*. She had worked hard to be
offered the part, since she was not originally
even under consideration. Andrew Lloyd
Webber had wanted an actress of Spanish
descent, and both Meryl Streep and Michelle
Pfeiffer had also been considered. The movie
featured three songs that Madonna went on to
release as singles: "You Must Love Me,"
"Don't Cry For Me Argentina," and "Another
Suitcase In Another Hall." "You Must Love
Me" was a new song that was not included on
the original stage version of *Evita*, having been
written after director Alan Parker requested
changes in the story towards the end.

A most fashionable artist...

Opposite and right: Madonna at the 1st annual VH1 Fashion & Music Awards, which were held at Lexington Avenue Armory in Manhattan, New York City. She presented the Fashion's Future award to Gucci's Tom Ford and received the Most Fashionable Artist award from her ex-husband Sean Penn. Although the two of them had been divorced for nearly seven years, many felt that there was still a feeling of "unfinished business" between them. According to some reports, Penn continued to believe that they were doomed always to love each other even though they apparently couldn't make their marriage work.

Meanwhile, Madonna was still involved with Carlos Leon, and had begun to plan a future that would involve him long term. According to her brother Christopher, she now desperately wanted to have a baby and had decided that Leon was the ideal person to be the father.

October 1996: Baby Lourdes

Left: Madonna seen out and about in Manhattan. Filming for *Evita* was due to start in February 1996, with locations in England, Hungary, Spain, and Argentina.

Around halfway through the schedule, Madonna discovered that she was pregnant with her first child, by Carlos Leon. Lourdes Maria Ciccone Leon was born on October 14 at the Good Samaritan Hospital in Los Angeles, California. The new arrival weighed in at a healthy 6lb 9oz. Madonna later said that the birth had marked a turning point for her, making her look at life in a way she never had before. Only two months later, in December, Madonna had also been presented with a Lifetime Achievement Award at the *Billboard* Music Awards ceremony in Las Vegas, Nevada, in her first public appearance since the birth of her daughter.

Opposite: With David Byrne of Talking Heads at the 11th annual Rock and Roll Hall of Fame induction dinner, which was held at the Waldorf-Astoria hotel in New York City. The inductees were David Bowie, Gladys Knight and the Pips, Jefferson Airplane, Pink Floyd, the Shirelles, and the Velvet Underground. Madonna accepted his award on behalf of David Bowie, who was unable to attend.

December 1995: Evita

Opposite and right: Madonna attends the première of *Evita* in Los Angeles wearing an outfit inspired by the fashion of Eva Peron. In the film Madonna wears 85 different costumes, which outdid the previous record of 65 costume changes held by Elizabeth Taylor in the 1963 film *Cleopatra*.

In general the critics received the movie well: a review in *Total Film* reported, "Remarkable, gloriously realized and exceedingly large-scale movie version of the celebrated 1970s stage musical, notable for brilliant performances from Madonna and the glossy-eyebrowed Banderas, spectacular set-piece scenes and an incredible true story," while a reviewer for the *Los Angeles Daily News* thought: "The woman who made a career of reinventing herself—from Disco Diva to Virtual Virgin to Sexual Shocker—has done it again. She has transformed herself into a musical theater star, sliding into that precious zone where rock stars dare not travel."

You must love me...

Opposite: Madonna at a press conference for *Evita* in London. The general consensus of opinion—even from Madonna's sternest critics—was that with this movie she had finally proved that she could act as well as sing. The style of *Evita* also started a new fashion for 1940s era clothes and makeup, so yet again Madonna was instigating a new trend.

Above: A scene from the movie. In Argentina, Madonna and the film crew had been confronted with angry protests and demonstrations by people afraid that Madonna would tarnish the reputation of Eva Peron. However, President Carlos Menem gave his blessing for them to film the famous balcony scene for the song, "Don't Cry For Me Argentina" from the actual balcony at Casa Rosada.

Golden Globe January 1997

Left and opposite: At the Golden Globe Awards in January 1997 with Carlos Leon (left) and Nicole Kidman (opposite). Nicole Kidman presented Madonna with the Best Actress in a Musical or Comedy award for her performance in *Evita*. During her acceptance speech Madonna described the experience of working on the movie as "an incredible adventure." The movie also won Best Motion Picture—Musical or Comedy, and Best Original Song for "You Must Love Me."

In March there was another award: at the 69th annual Academy Awards in Los Angeles, Madonna performed "You Must Love Me" and the song won the Oscar for Best Original Song.

Over the next few months, Madonna cut back on her public appearances to enable her to spend some time with her new daughter. She also ended her romantic relationship with Carlos Leon later that spring, although the two of them remained close friends and he continued to see his daughter regularly.

New beliefs

Above: Madonna with Kate Moss and Donatella Versace at a Versace Gala in August 1997. Madonna is wearing a red string around her wrist to ward off the "evil eye"—she had recently developed an interest in Kabbalah after being introduced to it by her friend, comedian and actress Sandra Bernhard. Followers believe that the path to spiritual enlightenment lies in a mix of Orthodox Jewish tradition and positive thinking. Rabbi Philip Berg founded the first branch of the Kabbalah Center in Jerusalem in 1969 and the organization now has centers around the world. Madonna adopted the Hebrew name Esther among followers and donates several million pounds each year. Her involvement with Kabbalah has raised its profile around the world. Some investigative journalists have claimed that followers are pressured into donating large sums of money, but Madonna has been a staunch defender, saying: "It frightens people, so they try to denigrate it or trivialize it so that it makes more sense." In some interviews she has spoken about how studying the teachings of Kabbalah has "changed my whole outlook on life."

Ray of Light

Opposite: Madonna appears on CBS-TV's *The Rosie O'Donnell Show* to promote her new single, "Frozen," from the new album, *Ray of Light*. "Frozen" went on to become a major hit for her all over the world and is often considered to be one of Madonna's best songs. It features Middle Eastern undertones and electronic sounds as well as a new vocal range for Madonna herself—since training for *Evita* had strengthened her voice—and was quite a radical change in style from her previous work. It entered the U.K. charts at No. 1 and reached the top in many other countries too, although in the U.S. it didn't manage to knock Céline Dion's "My Heart Will Go On" off the top spot in the *Billboard* Hot 100 chart. Madonna did a short promotional tour around Europe to promote *Ray of Light*, with scheduled appearances in London in England, San Remo in Italy, Paris in France, Duisberg In Germany, and Madrid in Spain.

Right: Accompanied by her brother Christopher on the red carpet at the 1998 Academy Awards.

A music masterpiece

Opposite: A still from the *Ray of Light* video, which was shot in Los Angeles and New York City and directed by Jonas Akerlund. The album itself was produced by Patrick Leonard and William Orbit and features Orbit's distinctive electronic music, which Madonna admired. The lyrics reveal Madonna's new-found spirituality and joy in motherhood, and the music has a different sound, which Madonna described as "techno-music made emotional and intimate." She also publicly gave credit to the Kabbalah Center for its "creative guidance." The album was praised as her best work yet—the critics called it "a music masterpiece of the decade." Reviewers commented that it was Madonna's "most adventurous" record to date and lauded its more mature style. The songs appealed to audiences everywhere, earning her many new young fans in addition to the faithful who had followed her career to date. It went to the No. 1 spot in the U.K., mainland Europe, Canada, Australia, and New Zealand, but after debuting at No. 2 in the U.S. charts did not make it any higher.

Left: Singing at the Annual Rainforest Benefit.

September 1998: The Power of Goodbye

Above and opposite: Stills from the music video for "The Power of Goodbye," which was filmed in August 1998 at Silvertop House in Los Angeles and at Malibu Beach. The single "The Power of Goodbye" did quite well, although not as well as some of the others that had come from the *Ray of Light* album. Madonna had recently spoken openly about her newfound devotion to Kabbalah and credited it for helping her to develop her new trusting, humble, and kinder self.

It was also around this time that Madonna attended a party thrown by Sting, and the singer's wife, Trudie Styler, introduced her to British film director Guy Ritchie. Madonna was still involved with English writer Andy Bird, whom she had met 6 months previously, and Ritchie was seeing TV presenter Tania Strecker, but despite this the two of them hit it off immediately.

Six wins at the MTV Video Music Awards

Left: With Jonas Akerlund, who directed the video for "Ray of Light," at the 15th annual MTV Video Music Awards held in Los Angeles, California, on September 10, 1998. "Ray of Light" won five awards: Video of the Year, Best Female Video, Best Directing, Best Choreography, and Best Editing. On the same day it was also certified gold in the U.S., having sold 500,000 copies. The video for "Frozen," directed by Chris Cunningham, won Best Special Effects. During the program Madonna performed "Ray of Light" and also "Shanti/Ashtangi"; the World Vaishnava Association (WVA) later condemned her performance as sacrilegious because she wore a holy facial marking coupled with a see-through blouse—but Madonna's response was that "essence of purity and divinity is non-judgment." Meanwhile, the new video for "The Power of Goodbye" premièred on MTV, the day after the awards were broadcast.

Opposite: With Geri Halliwell, who had recently left the Spice Girls to launch her solo career.

Around this time Madonna also developed a passion for yoga as part of her workout routine. Her amazing shape and energy, as well as her serene new outlook on life, were commented on in the press and soon began to trigger a new fitness trend.

Boundless energy and creativity

Opposite and right: At the 4th annual
VH1 Fashion Awards, which were held
at Madison Square Garden in New
York City on October 23. Madonna
performed "The Power Of Goodbye,"
which had debuted at No. 6 in the U.K.
singles chart and stayed there for nine
weeks. In the U.S. it missed the Top
Ten, peaking at No. 11. She also
became the first recipient of the Gianni
Versace Tribute Award, which had been
newly created by VH1 to pay tribute to
the late designer Gianni Versace, and
would be presented each year to "the
person who best continues to
represent the boundless energy, infinite
creativity, and fearlessness that was
Versace." In addition, this year she also
won the award for Most Fashionable
Female Artist as well as the Most
Stylish Music Artist.

The eye-catching yellow gown (right)
that Madonna wore for part of the
awards ceremony was designed by up-
and-coming designer Ollvier
Theyskens, who went on to head the
fashion house of Rochas.

November 1998: MTV Europe Music Awards

Opposite and right: Madonna continued her run of success at the 5th annual MTV Europe Music Awards, collecting the award for Best Female Artist and Best Album, for *Ray of Light*. Unlike the main MTV video music awards, winners of the European awards are mainly voted for by viewers, so winning here was a real indication of how Madonna had succeeded in moving away from the controversy and completely changing her image to win back and even extend her core audience. She performed "The Power of Goodbye" at the awards ceremony, which was broadcast live from Milan, Italy, on November 13.

While recording the album *Ray of Light* Madonna had taken pronunciation lessons from eminent Sanskrit scholar Dr. Vagish Sashtri to enable her to pronounce the Sanskrit shlokas—rhythmic poetic verses, which are similar to hymns—on the album correctly.

Fire and Ice

Left and opposite: At the 9th annual Fire & Ice Ball at Universal Studios, Los Angeles, with supermodel Naomi Campbell (left) and Donatella Versace (opposite). The event featured Donatella Versace's 1999 collection, and Madonna wore a stunning Versace backless dress with a diagonal slashes from neck to toe, a high neck, and an unusual fringed trim. The Fire & Ice ball was initiated in 1990 and is held annually to benefit the Revlon/UCLA Women's Cancer Research Program.

A few days later, *Ray of Light* was certified 3 x platinum in the U.S. having sold 3 million copies. Later that month Madonna won Top Dance Club Play Artist and Top Dance Club Play Single for "Ray of Light" in the *Billboard* Music Awards, while in Denmark she was named Most Popular Artist and *Ray of Light* Most Popular Album of 1998. It brought to an end one of her most successful years to date.

Grammy winner

Right Madonna performing a Japanese-styled "Nothing Really Matters" at the 41st annual Grammy Awards in Los Angeles on February 24, 1999.

Opposite: "Ray of Light" had been nominated for 6 Grammy Awards and won four of them: Best Pop Album, Best Dance Recording, Best Recording Package and Best Short-Form Music Video. It missed out only on Album Of The Year and Record Of The Year, but was still a career best for her. She had also recently won Best International Female Artist and Best International Album for *Ray of Light* at the 10th annual Dansk Grammy Awards held at Tivoli's Garden Concert Hall in Copenhagen, Denmark.

Meanwhile Madonna had signed a long-term licensing and marketing contract with Sony Signatures to lend her name and image to fashion designers and manufacturers of fragrances, cosmetics, and collectibles. The first result of this was a $6.5 million agreement with Max Factor to collaborate on a line of several new cosmetic products, and to appear in advertising campaigns that would run in Europe, Japan, and Asia.

Battling against AIDS

Opposite: Madonna arriving at the *Vanity Fair* post-Academy Awards party, which was held at Morton's restaurant in West Hollywood, California, on March 21. In her personal life, Madonna's friendship with British film director Guy Ritchie was still quietly developing behind the scenes. The press had not yet picked up on their relationship, and in February she attended the Los Angeles premiere of his new film, *Lock, Stock And Two Smoking Barrels*.

Above: Dr. Mathilde Krim, David Granger, editor of *Esquire*, and Madonna at a reception to launch the March issue of the magazine. It had a major feature about the AIDS crisis, and used celebrity AIDS activists to call attention to the problem. The gatefold cover had a photograph by Patrick Demarchelier of Madonna along with other stars, including Tom Hanks, Lauryn Hill and Sharon Stone, each holding up a placard to read: The Four Letter Word We All Forgot About.

Kindred spirits

Opposite: Madonna with her friend the British actor
Rupert Everett study the new range at a Versace
fashion show. The two of them had recently been
filming a movie, *The Next Best Thing*, on location in
California.

In June Madonna had released her new single,
"Beautiful Stranger," an up-tempo love song that had
been written for the soundtrack to the Austin Powers
sequel *The Spy Who Shagged Me*. In the U.S. it was
released only on the movie soundtrack album, but still
made No. 19 in the *Billboard* Hot 100 purely on the
strength of airplay. It also reached No. 1 in the Hot
Dance Music/Club Play chart and No. 3 on the Hot
Dance Singles Sales charts. In the U.K. it became one
of the most played songs on the radio ever, making
Madonna the first female solo artist to top the Radio
Airplay chart in England, and reached No. 2 in the
singles charts. It went on to sell 4.5 million copies
worldwide. The video featured Mike Myers as Austin
Powers, trying to catch a spy in disguise who turns out
to be Madonna. However, fans were disappointed to
learn that she had no plans to tour again in the
immediate future.

Right: With Demi Moore at the launch of *Talk*
magazine on Liberty Island, Manhattan, in August
1999. Demi Moore was also a staunch devotee of
Kabbalah and the two of them later hosted a launch
party for Rabbi Philip Berg's new book.

A date with Paul McCartney

Above and opposite: With Paul McCartney at the 16th annual MTV Video Music Awards, which were held at the Metropolitan Opera House, New York City, on September 9. They co-presented the Best Video Of The Year award to Lauryn Hill for "Doo Wop (That Thing.") Madonna herself won Best Video From A Film for "Beautiful Stranger." MTV also staged a tribute to her as the Most Honored Artist Of The 20th Century in the 15-year history of the MTV Video Music Awards—with a career total of 18 awards—presenting a series of male drag artists dressed as the singer in her past music videos. For once Madonna was not the source of controversy—this time it was Lil' Kim, who wore an outfit that exposed one breast.In October, Madonna traveled to London to begin work on her new album. Just before she left the U.S. on *Concorde*, British Airways staff received a threatening phone call concerning her. When the plane arrived at Terminal Four of Heathrow Airport, a hastily arranged security operation led to Madonna being flanked by six uniformed officers and a police dog as she carried Lourdes from the plane, through the baggage hall and out to her limousine. In the event there was no incident, but this was not the first or the last time that Madonna was plagued by obsessive fans, or received death threats.

Fashionable friends

Left: Madonna at the 5th annual VH1/Vogue Fashion Awards at the Lexington Avenue Armory, Manhattan on December 5. It was the first time that style maker *Vogue* magazine had collaborated in the awards, giving them new credibility. Madonna presented the Male Celebrity Style Award to Rupert Everett. She had been nominated for Most Fashionable Female Artist, but had lost out to Jennifer Lopez. Several presenters jokingly referred to copies of *Vogue* magazine or *The New York Post* newspaper instead of using the official award envelopes, after the magazine accidentally went out too early and *The Post* published a list of the winners the day before the show.

Opposite: With Rupert Everett and Stella McCartney at the awards. Madonna had been close friends with Stella since the late 1990s, after buying some clothes from her. In a British newspaper interview about their first meeting, Stella said, "Madonna came to my studio in London when I just had left college. I was running a bath and was totally unprepared. I thought, 'Oh my God she's here'—panicked and ran downstairs to let her in. There were paparazzi everywhere taking her picture, which really flustered me. When I ran back upstairs the bath had over run and had started to flood my flat. It was a nightmare! Then, when she tried my clothes on, I told her she had a fat arse. She laughed... and bought some."

December 1999: A new life dawns

Opposite: Madonna with Stella McCartney.

Right: Madonna and Guy Ritchie were spotted together in Central Park on Christmas Day 1999. They also celebrated the dawn of the new millennium at Donatella Versace's party at the Versace Mansion in Miami, Florida. Early in 2000 news broke that Madonna was pregnant for a second time, and that the father was Guy Ritchie—the story appeared for the first time on *The Sun* newspaper's website, and press interest in the couple's relationship quickly escalated. It was also soon noted that Madonna had begun to spend increasing amounts of her time in the U.K.

In November 1999, Madonna released a video of some her favorite music videos, which was called *Madonna: The Video Collection 93–99*. Originally it had been planned to cover 1992–99 and was to feature "Erotica," but in an effort to be less controversial this was replaced with "The Power of Goodbye" instead. Madonna also featured several times in *Billboard* magazine's Totally 90s—Diary Of A Decade: at No. 6 in Top Pop Artist Of The Decade; at No. 4 in Top Pop Female Artist Of The Decade; and reaching No. 24 with "Take A Bow" and No. 93 with "Vogue" in the Hot 100 Singles Of The Decade.

The Next Best Thing

Left and opposite: Stills from *The Next Best Thing*, a comedy drama directed by John Schlesinger, which was released in March 2000. In the movie, Madonna plays yoga teacher Abbie, who—despairing of finding the perfect partner—has a one night stand with her gay best friend, played by Rupert Everett, that results in the birth of a child. The two of them agree to bring up the boy together, but then she meets a new man and wants to move away with him and the child, leading to a nasty custody battle.

Madonna arrived at Leicester Square in London for the U.K. première on June 6 heavily pregnant with her second child and accompanied by Guy Ritchie. She delighted waiting fans by looking very glamorous but chatting easily to everyone. She joked with journalists that "life imitates art sometimes" because her character in the film is also pregnant unexpectedly.

A new version of American Pie

Opposite: Guy Ritchie and Madonna at the party after the London première of *The Next Best Thing*. The soundtrack of the movie featured a cover of the Don McLean classic, "American Pie," which Madonna sings backed by Rupert Everett. It is much shorter than the original version, but still quickly climbed the charts, reaching No. 1 in several countries around the world including the U.K., Australia, and Japan. It wasn't released as a single in the U.S., but still reached No. 29 in the *Billboard* Hot 100 on airplay alone. Madonna was executive producer for the soundtrack album, picking all the songs to be featured and including tracks by Christina Aguilera and Beth Orton. It only had one other sung by Madonna herself, "Time Stood Still," a new song that she had written with William Orbit, which was not released as a single. The album peaked at No. 34 on the *Billboard* 200.

Right: With Sting at an aftershow party. Madonna and Sting had been friends since the late 1990s, when she spent time at his Tuscan home. Sting and his wife Trudie had become friendly with Guy Ritchie during the filming of his 1998 movie *Lock, Stock, and Two Smoking Barrels*—on which Styler was Executive Producer.

August 2000: Rocco arrives

Madonna had decided to give birth in the U.S., after condemning U.K. hospitals as old, Victorian, and inefficient. She went into labor three weeks prematurely and was rushed to Cedars Sinai Hospital in Los Angeles, late on August 10. After problems with the birth and concerns for the health of the baby she was eventually given an emergency Cesarean and her first son arrived just after midday on August 11.

Baby Rocco Ritchie was small at 5lb 9oz and had to be placed into intensive care for several days for observation, but was otherwise fit and healthy. Madonna left the hospital ahead of her son, but returned daily to be at his bedside. He was finally released from hospital to go home on Madonna's birthday, August 16.

September 2000: Major success for Music

Left and opposite: Madonna makes a surprise in-store appearance at the Virgin Megastore in West Hollywood, California, to sign copies of her newly-released album *Music*. Critics had applauded the new album and some believed it was even better than *Ray of Light*, since the underlying tone of the tracks was one of happiness—reflecting Madonna's new state of mind after the birth of her son and the development of her relationship with Ritchie. The album sold 420,000 copies in one week in the U.S. and reached No. 1 in 23 different countries, including the U.S., where it was her first No. 1 album for 11 years. Madonna's brand new rhinestone-clad "urban cowgirl" image—coupled with a head of tumbling gold locks—also set a trend for cowboy hats and boots across the world.

In August Madonna had become the first female solo artist to have ten No. 1 singles in the U.K. when the single of "Music" reached the top spot. It was her 12th No. 1 in the U.S., making her only the second artist in the U.S. to have achieved a No. 1 in the 1980s, 1990s and the 2000s. The video of the song, directed by Jonas Akerlund, went on to reach No. 3 in the U.S. on the *Billboard* Top Music Videos chart.

Broadcasting around the world

Opposite: Performing "Music" at the 7th
annual MTV Europe Music Awards, held at
the Globe Arena in Stockholm, Sweden on
November 16 and broadcast live around the
world. She appeared in front of a large screen
projecting images from her 18-year career,
wearing a torn black T-shirt held together with
diamond-encrusted safety pins and with the
Australian singer Kylie Minogue's name
across the front. The song itself carried on
collecting awards, being named Single Of The
Year by *People* magazine the following month,
as well as being voted Best Pop Single and
Best Pop Album in the annual Dotmusic.com
Records Of The Year readers' poll.

Right: Madonna won Best Female and Best
Dance at the MTV Europe Music Awards, but
lost out on Best Song to "Rock DJ" by Robbie
Williams. She had also recently been awarded
Best International Female Artist at the 4th
annual Premios Amigo Awards in Madrid,
Spain.

Meanwhile, Madonna was preparing to
start a new life based in England. In
November she purchased a £10 million
Georgian house in London's Belgravia area,
and in December it was announced that she
and Guy Ritchie were engaged and would
marry in December in Scotland.

December 2000: Celebrations

Left: On the evening of December 21, more than a thousand fans gathered outside the small, 776-year-old cathedral at Dornoch in Scotland to see Madonna and Guy Ritchie arrive for the christening of their baby son. Inside, the church was lit with candles and garlanded with ivy and flowers; Rocco wore a $45,000 Versace white-and-gold christening outfit, a gift from Donatella Versace. After the service, the proud parents posed on the steps of the cathedral for photographs with their baby, before speeding off back to Skibo Castle for their wedding. It was the last the press would see of them until the five-day wedding celebrations were over.

Fairy tale wedding

Above: In an attempt to stop unauthorized photos of the wedding of the year being published, none of the guests was allowed a mobile phone and they were all banned from leaving the castle. The ceremony was held in the Great Hall, lit by candles, and garlanded in ivy and white orchids. Lourdes, in a long ivory high-necked dress, descended the staircase first scattering red rose petals. Madonna looked beautiful in a fitted Gothic-style ivory silk dress, designed by Stella McCartney, and set off with antique French jewelry. Guy wore a kilt in the plaid of the Mackintosh clan, while Rocco was dressed in a kilt of identical fabric. After the celebrations were over, Madonna and her husband left for a short honeymoon at the Wiltshire estate of Sting and Trudie Styler.

Part Three

Nobody Knows Me

Mrs Ritchie

Opposite: Mr and Mrs Ritchie at the Los Angeles première of Ritchie's new film, *Snatch*, at the Directors Guild of America. Madonna's career was still on a roll: at the 2nd annual NRJ Music Awards at the MIDEM Music Conference held in Cannes, France, at the end of January, she won Best International Female Artist and Best International Album for Music. The same month she also won Best Single and Best Video for the single "Music" and the award for Best-Dressed Artist in *Rolling Stone* magazine's 25th annual readers' poll.

Above: In April 2001, Madonna released "What It Feels Like For A Girl" from the album *Music*, with a controversial music video directed by her husband. It featured Madonna going on a dangerous joy ride, accompanied by an elderly woman, in which she robs a man, threatens police officers with a water pistol, sets a gas station alight, and finally appears to commit suicide. It was condemned for being overly violent and banned from being shown on most U.S. and European TV channels except late at night—even though it was no more violent than many TV shows.

Embarking on a new tour

Opposite and above: In February Madonna had announced that she was planning a new tour, her first for eight years. The Drowned World tour was supposed to begin on June 5 in Cologne, Germany, but technical difficulties meant these shows had to be canceled. It eventually started on June 9 in Barcelona, Spain, and ended on September 15 in Los Angeles. The tour was scheduled to visit only cities in Europe and the U.S., which disappointed many fans, but Madonna appeared to want a tight travel plan now she had a young family. In U.K., the tour broke box-office records for a fastest-selling concert at Earls Court, London, when 16,000 tickets for the July 4 concert were sold out in only 15 minutes. A further 80,000 tickets for an extra five dates were sold out in only six hours, and tickets changed hands on the black market for more than £2,000 each. In France and Germany, tickets for two concerts were sold out in only 30 minutes. The playlist for the tour was based on Madonna's recent work, with "La Isla Bonita" and "Holiday" included from the 80s. Costume changes included a punk rock look with a tartan kilt, a rhinestone cowboy outfit, a Japanese-themed gown and a gangster/ghetto girl look.

A response to 9/11

Opposite and right: In the last section of the show, Madonna performed "Music" wearing a customized Dolce and Gabbana T shirt that read Mother on the front and F☆cker on the back.

The show that had been scheduled to take place at the Staples Center in Los Angeles on September 11 was canceled after the terrorist attack on the Twin Towers in New York, but a new show was scheduled for September 15 instead. Slight changes were made to the shows after the attack: for these last few appearances Madonna wore an American Flag-kilt during the opening segment, and some of the more violent sections and songs were dropped. She donated proceeds from some of the shows for the children of the victims of the 9/11 attack, becoming one of the first celebrities to donate money.

The tour was a massive success, and even critics who were disapproving of some of Madonna's past behavior found something to praise. The *New Musical Express* said, "Her voice sounded fuller and smoother than previous tours, and she confidently exposed it in the ballads 'You'll See' and 'I Deserve It,' post-breakup songs that insist she'll recover. She picked up a guitar every so often, playing a punk girl at one point and a country gal (singing a ditty about cannibalism with a put-on Southern drawl) later. And while she danced more sparingly than she had in previous tours, she still made herself an object of authority and desire."

The greatest hits...

Left and opposite: On stage during the Drowned World tour. The show that had been scheduled to take place on August 3 in New Jersey had to be canceled because Madonna was having problems with her throat. On the very last day of the tour, on September 15 in Los Angeles, Guy Ritchie surprised her by appearing on stage as the lost technician at the end of "Beautiful Stranger"—he had also appeared unexpectedly to present her with a birthday cake at the end of the show in Miami, on August 15.

Just after the tour finished, Madonna released *GHV2*, a compilation album of her greatest hits. In an interview with Jo Whiley on U.K. television's BBC channel, she was asked about how the songs for the album had been selected and said, "I only wanted songs that I could listen to five times in a row." To avoid a label of "explicit lyrics," some of the songs were edited down to remove swear words or sexual references. The album did not contain any new material—only previously released material was included—and there was not to be another new single until October 2002. The "material girl" was too busy settling into her new life in Britain to make music—she and her husband had recently bought the 1,200-acre Ashcombe estate in Wiltshire, formerly owned by Sir Cecil Beaton, for £9 million. The estate included established shooting moors and Ritchie was a crack shot. Encouraged by her husband, Madonna took private shooting lessons with top gunsmiths Holland and Holland and also became interested in several other country pursuits, such as horse riding.

Swept Away

Opposite: A still from the movie *Swept Away*, directed by Guy Ritchie and starring Madonna as a rich, spoiled socialite who is stranded on a desert island with a sailor. Filming began on location in Sardinia, Malta, and Italy only a few weeks after the Drowned World tour finished. When it was released in October 2002, *Swept Away* was pulled from many cinemas in the U.S. after only a few weeks and went straight to video in the U.K. However, one critic commented that Madonna had given her best performance ever. The soundtrack did not feature any Madonna songs, although there were some by other artists. Earlier in the year Madonna had also starred in a $1.4 million, 7-minute commercial for BMW cars, *Star*, which was also directed by her husband.

Left: Madonna on stage in Los Angeles during the Drowned World tour.

A new life in Britain

Left: Madonna with daughter Lourdes, now nearly six years old. The family was now based in Britain, with a £5.7 million town house in London as well as the Ashcombe House estate in Wiltshire. The London house was undergoing extensive renovation—and Madonna caused a storm of criticism in the British press when she complained during an interview that British workmen worked far fewer hours than their American counterparts.

Opposite: With Donatella Versace and American actress Gwyneth Paltrow at a showing of the new Versace collection at the Trocadero Center in Paris on January 19, 2002. Madonna and Paltrow had been friends for several years—a friendship that was cemented after Paltrow married Coldplay lead singer Chris Martin the following year and also became based in the U.K. The February issue of U.K.'s *Heat* magazine featured several photographs of stars at the Versace event—but the *Daily Mail* had recently started a serialization of screenwriter Andy Bird's story of his love affair with Madonna in 1998.

The same month, at the 36th annual MIDEM Music Conference held in Cannes, France, Madonna was named the second best-selling artist in Europe by the International Federation Of The Phonographic Industry, having received 17 platinum Europe awards over five of her albums.

A private view

Opposite: Lourdes, Madonna, and Guy Ritchie arrive for the private view and launch party for the Mario Testino exhibition on January 29 at the National Portrait Gallery in London. The display was open to the public from February 1 to June 4. The exhibition featured more than 120 color and black-and-white photographs by Testino, including several of Madonna. Testino had pictured the singer for a 1995 Versace campaign, and in 1997 took the shot for the cover of her *Ray of Light* album. In an interview, he spoke about the first time he had worked with Madonna: "When Madonna first came to meet me in a hotel I said, 'My God, I have never seen you like this without makeup!' Before, you know, I had only ever seen her being the tough girl, or Marilyn, or the rock chick. Instead she came in looking very natural, no makeup, flat shoes, and ponytail. So I said: 'Can I photograph you like this? See who the Madonna without foundation is?' She agreed, but when I showed her the photographs before retouching she was, like, 'Oh my God, people don't want to see me like this.' I showed them to her again after I had done a little retouching and she was happy. She understood what I was trying to do without the makeup."

A West End debut

Opposite: The Ritchie family enjoy a day out in the early spring sunshine in Hyde Park in London. In May, Madonna made her London West End theater debut, playing art dealer Loren in *Up For Grabs*, written by renowned Australian playwright David Williamson. The first night was delayed for three days because of technical difficulties with the staging which involved a two-tiered glass box whose lower panels slid sleekly back and forth to indicate shifting locations. On the opening night a technical hitch caused the moving set to grind to a halt about 15 minutes into the play, at the start of a scene between Madonna's character Loren and her stage husband Tom Irwin. Madonna and Irwin

managed to carry on the scene at the front of the stage without appearing to be affected at all, and after the scene was completed the curtain came down for a ten minute interval so the scenery could be fixed. A review in *Heat* magazine said, "...from the moment the curtain rose to reveal Mrs Ritchie standing before us, a pair of razor-sharp stilettos on her feet and a faint smile across her lips, she had us in the palm of her hand." Madonna later won the Theater Event Of The Year in the whatsonstage.com Theatregoers' Choice Awards.

Above: Madonna and Guy Richie attend a screening of *Swept Away*.

Bond girl

Left and opposite: Madonna and Guy Ritchie with Pierce Brosnan at the London première of the new James Bond movie, *Die Another Day*. Madonna played Bond's fencing instructor, Verity, in a cameo role; her scene takes place in the Blades Club in London, and involves her supervising Bond as he duels with arch-villain Gustav Graves. Her part was originally supposed to be longer, but other commitments meant she could not spare more time for filming. Madonna also sang the movie's theme song, which she released as a single in October 2002 and which went on to be nominated for a Golden Globe Award for Best Original Song. The song peaked at No. 1 in 12 different countries, including an eight-week stint in the top spot on the World Music Charts, and an 11-week stay at No. 1 in the *Billboard* Hot 100 chart—a record for Madonna.

In the *Rolling Stone* magazine list of Top 100 Albums Of All Time in October 2002, Madonna had more albums on the list than any other female solo artist: *Ray of Light* at No. 29, *Music* at No. 52, *Like A Prayer* at No. 62, and *The Immaculate Collection* at No. 99.

A royal première

Above: Madonna shares a joke with Rosamund Pike, Rick Yune, and John Cleese as they wait backstage to be presented to Her Majesty Queen Elizabeth II and Prince Philip at the royal première screening of *Die Another Day*. The Royal Albert Hall had been transformed into a glittering ice palace for the screening, just like the lair of the villain in the film.

A moment to remember

Above: Madonna was dressed conservatively in a long, black cocktail dress and took the time to make sure she knew how to greet the Queen. She practiced her curtsey in front of co-star John Cleese (opposite), and afterward said, "The queen asked me about Bond. I have never met her before, but surprisingly I wasn't nervous." Proceeds from première, of about £500,000, were donated to the Cinema and Television Benevolent Fund of which the Queen was patron.

American Life

Above and opposite: Madonna performs songs from her ninth studio album, *American Life*, at MTV studios in April. The album was released on April 22 and its theme was American society and materialism. Although it was hailed by music critics as moving in an exciting new direction for Madonna, it did not do as well commercially as some of her other albums. The title song, released as a single earlier in the month, had peaked at No. 37 on the *Billboard* Hot 100—possibly because its anti-war theme was seen as unpatriotic at a time America was at war

with Iraq. At the beginning of April Madonna had announced on her official website that she had canceled the release of the music video for the single "American Life" out of sensitivity and respect for the armed forces. The video had been filmed before war broke out in Iraq, and was filled with military imagery, which she had come to feel might be misinterpreted by some people. She subsequently filmed a new performance-only version of the song.

Think like me

Above and opposite: Madonna meets several members of the New York City Fire Department during an in-store appearance at Tower Records in downtown New York City on April 23, to promote her new CD *American Life*. During the appearance she performed "American Life," "Mother and Father," "X-Static Process," "Nothing Fails," "Like A Virgin," and "Hollywood," and signed copies of her CD. In an interview in *People* magazine to promote American Life, she said, "I've grown. I don't want people to dress like me anymore... I want them to think like me. Dress like Britney Spears and think like me—and everything will be fine."

Guest of honor

Opposite: On May 15, Madonna was guest of honor for the opening of her close friend Stella McCartney's first London shop in Bruton Street, Mayfair. A while ago Melly and Stelly—as they reportedly called each other—had fallen out over Madonna's fondness for wearing fur, but they had since made up and Madonna wore a satin raincoat to the event. After the party, McCartney, her fiance Alasdhair Willis, Madonna and her husband Guy Ritchie went out for dinner and then on to a nightclub.

Right: Madonna at the launch of a new book by Kabbalah founder Rabbi Philip Berg on April 24. The following month, on May 9, she made her first-ever U.K. in-store appearance at London's HMV on Oxford Street. Five hundred lucky fans had lined up the previous day to get the elusive tickets that would allow them in to see Madonna. She performed a seven-song set, with a full band including French dance music supremo Mirwais Ahmadzaim, who produced *American Life*.

Feeling revolutionary

Left: Madonna performing "Hollywood" on BBC television's *Top of the Pops* in May. In many of the publicity photographs for *American Life* she is wearing a beret and some pictures are almost a copy of the iconic image of Che Guevara. In an interview to promote the Italian version of *Top of the Pops* Madonna said that the choice to emulate Che's image had been deliberate because she liked what he represented and was feeling revolutionary when she wrote the songs for the album.

Meanwhile, Madonna had put her Beverly Hills home on the market for £7 million. She had bought the 1920s Mediterranean-style property just three years previously from actress Diane Keaton. Although she was now based in the U.K.—and her two children were at school there—she told reporters that she still intended to divide her time between the U.S. and the U.K. She soon bought a new U.S. home: a $13 million French Regency design home on Sunset Boulevard near the Beverly Hills Hotel, complete with a tennis court.

The face of Gap

Opposite: Madame Tussaud's in New York unveils a new figure of Madonna. The forthcoming Jean-Paul Gaultier retrospective at London's Victoria and Albert Museum included the iconic conical bra costume he had made for Madonna to wear on her Blond Ambition tour in 1983. In an interview for the London *Evening Standard*, Gaultier mentioned that it was one of his favorite pieces and that the two had been firm friends since. "Madonna is fabulous. She is a fashion freak—*un monstre de mode*. I remember the first time I saw her on the TV singing 'Holiday', and I was thinking she was English. I couldn't think she was American to dress like that. And when I met her in the flesh I was not disappointed. She is not false. She is like a little girl, truly enjoying, truly spontaneous with her different looks."

Right: Missy Elliott and Madonna in a European advertising campaign for Gap, entitled Madonna and Missy Into The Hollywood Groove. GAP London celebrated the launch with an event at the London flagship store on Oxford Street, as did the main New York store. Customers who bought a pair of cords could get them monogrammed and received an "Into The Hollywood Groove" CD. Some customers waited up to four hours because the monogram—M for Madonna or Missy—required 8887 stitches and each pair of cords took at least seven minutes to sew.

Mother and daughter appearance...

Left: Madonna makes her first appearance at the 2003 MTV Video Music Awards dressed as a "bridegroom" all in black with long, black spike-heel boots. She appeared at the top of a giant wedding cake at the start of her performance, wearing a tail coat and top hat. As she descended from the cake she sang her latest release, "Hollywood."

Opposite: Seven-year-old Lourdes gets a taste of the catwalk, when she makes a brief appearance at the MTV Video Music Awards at Radio City Music Hall in New York City in August. She came on with a friend, the two of them dressed as a pair of flower girls at a wedding, scattering petals at the start of her mother's section of the show.

May 2003: Center stage at the MTV Video Music Awards

Above and opposite: Madonna performing during the MTV Awards with Britney Spears (left) and Christina Aguilera (right). The performance had begun with Spears, 21, making her entrance from the giant wedding cake on stage, demurely dressed in a long, white wedding gown. She was joined by Aguilera, 22, in a similar gown and then they both ripped off their dresses to reveal skimpy white lace outfits and knee-length white boots. The two of them then sang Madonna's hit "Like A Virgin" together, in a homage to Madonna's version that had been performed at the 1984 MTV VMAs—which had caused its own press controversy at the time. As they finished the song, Madonna emerged from the cake in her black "bridegroom" outfit to sing "Hollywood", discarding the top hat and tails she was wearing initially as she joined them both on the stage. Towards the end of her song, Madonna pulled off a lacy garter from Aguilera's right leg (opposite).

A sensational kiss...

In a stunning finale, Madonna gave Spears a passionate French kiss (opposite) and then kissed Aguilera on the lips (left). The apparently impromptu display momentarily shocked the audience into silence, before they recovered and roared their approval. Madonna then called rapper Missy Elliot to join them, and Missy sang some of her hit song "Work It."

The steamy kisses stole the limelight from every other performer and presenter at the event and were subsequently featured on the front page of many U.S. and U.K. newspapers. One MTV producer later said: "It was sensational, but I wonder what the good folk in places like Provo, Utah state, would make of it. Middle America is not gonna let this one go lightly." However, American comedian Chris Rock, who presented the show for the third time, said: "That kiss was good, but where was mine?" and Duran Duran singer Simon Le Bon said: "I wish it was me she was snogging." Some newspapers criticized Madonna for using shock tactics yet again—but later it was revealed that the kiss had been Britney's idea.

The English Roses

Left: Madonna with 18-month-old Jeremy Zorek at a book signing event organized by Barnes and Noble in New York. Madonna read her 48-page book to a group of small children and then handed out signed copies to the 250 winners of a lottery held by the book store. "I have children and I read to them every night, so it's a perfect extension of who I am," she said to those attending the event. "I think children need to read inspiring books."

Right: Madonna used her interest in the teachings of Kabbalah as the inspiration for her children's books, the first of which, *The English Roses*, was launched in September 2003 in 30 languages and more than 100 countries. Each of the tales had a strong moral tone, and warn against such evils as greed and envy. "In the first book, the lesson is about how destructive feelings of envy and jealousy are. And everybody feels it, not just little girls," said Madonna. She also mentioned that "writing *The English Roses* was tremendously liberating. I never felt the pressure of having to impress anybody." *The English Roses* quickly became the fastest-selling children's picture book of all time, selling more than 10,000 copies in the U.K. in its first week alone. And in the children's best-seller list it was second only to the fifth Harry Potter — selling just 110 copies fewer than JK Rowling's book in its first seven days.

Tonight with Jay Leno...

Opposite: Madonna appears onstage as a presenter during *Spankin'
New Music Week* on MTV's *Total Request Live* at the MTV Times Square
Studios on November 13. The previous month the new Britney Spears
single, "Me Against the Music," had been released, which also featured
Madonna singing—she appeared in the music video for the song as
well. "Me Against the Music" was an international success, reaching the
top five in several countries. In the U.K. it reached No. 2, and it was also
a major hit in Australia.

Above: On November 26, 2003 Madonna appeared on *The Tonight Show
With Jay Leno*, her first appearance on the show for 10 years. She talked
mostly about her latest children's book, *Mr Peabody's Apples*—which had
just been published—the money from which she was planning to give to
the Spirituality for Kids Foundation, an educational arm of the Los
Angeles Kabbalah Center. She also talked about her relationship with
Guy—and how they fought about the silly things in life—as well as
about her children, fame, sex, and makeup.

Mr Peabody's Apples— a new book

Above and opposite: Madonna's second children's book, *Mr. Peabody's Apples*, was published on November 10, almost exactly a month after the publication of *The English Roses*. It debuted at No. 1 on *The New York Times'* best-seller list three weeks later—just as the first book had done. For a children's book author to climb to the top of list with two consecutive books released in such quick succession represented a first in publishing history. The story shows children that what matters is the truth—not how things appear—and teaches an unforgettable lesson about how we must choose our words carefully to avoid causing harm to others. At one of the launch events, Madonna appeared at the Montclair Kimberly Academy in Monclair, New Jersey to read *Mr Peabody's Apples* to a group of children. During an interview to promote the book, the star, who once complained that her own childhood was "very repressive, very catholic," admitted she is very strict with her own children, banning them from watching TV. Instead, they are permitted just one video or DVD each week "as a treat."

January 2004: NRJ Music Awards

Left: Madonna made a brief appearance at the NRJ Music Awards in Cannes to accept a Lifetime Achievement award from Britney Spears. Wearing a demure green polka-dot dress, she thanked her fans in France for two decades of support. "My ambition may be American, and I may have married a Brit, but my heart belongs to France," Madonna told the audience and received a standing ovation.

January also marked the release of *Nobody Knows Me*, a book of rare and unseen shots of Madonna's life, available only to order for one month from Madonna's official website.

Opposite: Missy Elliott with Madonna at the Warner Brothers party after the 46th annual Grammy Awards at the Staples Center in Los Angeles on February 4. Madonna, wearing a hot-pink silk-satin Versace slip dress, had introduced a performance by Sting and Sean Paul during the event. At the time, the newspapers were full of speculation that Madonna had had a facelift or botox to achieve her smooth and youthful appearance—but her spokeswoman said, "Madonna is radiantly happy in her life and glows with joy. It's that simple. Who wouldn't be aglow being with Guy Ritchie on a daily basis?"

That same month an advert appeared on a professional dancers' website for dancers for a forthcoming Madonna tour. No official announcement of a tour had been made but rumors soon began circulating. Since the dancers were required from March for rehearsals and June to September for the tour and only needed to be able to work in Europe and America, it was fairly certain that the tour would follow a similar schedule to the Drowned World tour of 2001.

Summer 2003: Re-Invention Tour

Above and opposite: The Re-Invention world tour began on May 24 in Los Angeles and traveled round North America, England, Ireland, France, The Netherlands, and Portugal, finishing in Lisbon, Portugal, on September 14. It visited 20 cities with a total of 56 performed shows—and Madonna was seen by an estimated 880,000 fans. Reviews for the show were very positive: *Rolling Stone* magazine said, "After twenty years in the limelight, Madonna is expected to cause controversy and reinvent herself for every new tour. So for the May 24th Los Angeles opening of her Re-Invention world trek, Madonna did the most unexpected thing she could: She came back as a great concert singer... In the midst of a $1 million production, including a walkway that jutted

out from the stage and over the audience, massive moving video screens, a dozen dancers, a bagpipe player, a stunt skateboarder and a whole lot of emotionally charged anti-war imagery. The focus of the show was nevertheless on Madonna, and how she's matured into a truly great pop singer." A review in The *New York Times* said, "Unlike 2001's Drowned World tour, which was dark, often hostile, Re-Invention returns Madonna to the light. She looks as if she is having a good time." The show had five different segments—Baroque/Marie Antoinette, Military/Army, Circus/Cabaret, Acoustic and Scottish/ Tribal—and featured revised versions of many of Madonna's past hits as well as costumes by Jean-Paul Gaultier, Christian Lacroix, and Stella McCartney.

The Adventures of Abdi

Opposite: On November 11 2004, Madonna's latest children's book, *The Adventures of Abdi*, was published. Pupils from St Winifred's Junior School in Newstead Road, Lee, were invited to the launch at Selfridges department store in central London, and Madonna read the entire story to them. Afterwards she answered questions, then thanked headteacher Mark Corrigan for the youngsters' excellent behavior. He said: "The children were excited and nervous before the event but once we arrived Madonna soon made them feel at ease." The story followed Abdi on a fantastic journey into a magical world of ruthless rogues, savage snakes, and deadly dungeons, where he remembers the wise words of his mentor: "Everything we have been given in life is always for the best."

Right: Madonna, wearing a green and white print dress by designer Diane von Furstenberg, speaks during a Spirituality for Kids event on September 19, 2004, at the Kabbalah International Conference held in Tel Aviv, Israel. During her speech Madonna said that New York City was just as dangerous as Israel and that she would not wait another 10 years to visit again.

Mother figure

Opposite: Madonna spotted in Paris out shopping with her daughter. Lourdes, 7, was at a French school in London and Madonna said that hearing her daughter read a poem in French was one of the things that made her happiest these days. The whole family had recently been for a short vacation in Miami, during which they were pictured swimming in the sea and playing on the beach like any other family with young children. In a magazine interview, Madonna said of her marriage, "The last thing I thought I would do is marry some laddish, shooting, pubgoing nature lover—and the last thing he thought he was going to do was marry some cheeky girl from the Midwest who doesn't take no for an answer!"

Right: With son Rocco, now nearly 4, in New York. During the Chicago leg of the Re-Invention tour, Madonna had arranged for several of her relatives—including her father, Tony Ciccone, her brother Christopher, and several other siblings and Michigan-based cousins—to come for a family reunion at the hotel in which she was staying and Lourdes and Rocco were very excited to see their cousins, aunts, and uncles arriving. The hotel also housed a film crew, who were following the tour for a documentary.

Meanwhile the newspapers were filled with stories about Elton John having accused Madonna of lip syncing during her concerts—claiming that it was unfair to charge fans such a high ticket price if she wasn't actually going to sing live. Madonna's spokeswoman simply replied that of course she sang live at her shows, and Elton later apologized, saying that he had not meant to offend.

July 2005: Live 8

Above and opposite: Madonna onstage during her spectacular performance at the Live 8 concert in London. Birhan Woldu—a famine survivor saved by money raised by the first Live Aid concert—who appeared on stage at the start of Madonna's set, was intimidated by the worldwide audience watching until Madonna held her hand. Woldu said, "The crowd seemed to stretch for miles, but I'd been telling myself not to be nervous. There was just a huge picture of me as a child on the screen. That photo still upsets me. It was 20 years ago when both my mother and sister died. I knew I must be strong for them but when I walked on I could feel my body shaking. Then Madonna took my hand and looked into my eyes. The crowd roared and I realized the world wanted to save my continent. I felt myself grow stronger." Madonna began her set with "Like A Prayer," backed by a full choir, who—like the star and her band—were dressed completely in white. "Are you ready to start a revolution?" Madonna asked the crowd. "Are you ready to change the world?" After "Ray of Light" she finished with an extended version of "Music" bringing break-dancers to the stage and leading 200,000 fans in a singalong.

A gay icon

Opposite: With Sir Bob Geldolf at the 2005 MTV European Music Awards held in Lisbon on November 3. Madonna opened the show by appearing from a glitter ball in a leotard, to sing her new release, "Hung Up." During the show she presented Geldolf with the Free Your Mind Award for his tireless campaign against world hunger, saying "It's not always been considered fashionable to make the world a better place... I've taken some shit for that myself. You drive me crazy, you f**ker! I couldn't be more proud than at this moment to present this award."

Above: Appearing at the G-A-Y concert at the Astoria Theatre in London on November 19, in one of her most outstanding live shows. Her performance of "Let It Will Be" was one of the highlights of the night, with fantastic electronic images flashing on the catwalk. Madonna writhed and gave her all – the fans in the front row could even reach out and touch her. "Hung Up" had recently entered the U.K. singles chart at No. 1, Madonna's 54th Top 10 hit, and she had also just released her 18th album, *Confessions on a Dance Floor*.

I'm Going To Tell You A Secret

Opposite: Madonna had a serious horse-riding accident in August 2005, in which she suffered three cracked ribs, a broken collarbone and a broken hand. The accident happened when she was thrown from a horse in the grounds of her country home, Ashcombe House, on her 47th birthday. She was knocked unconscious and when she came round attempted to get up and passed out again. She was treated at hospital in Salisbury, 90 miles south-west of London but was a terrible patient as nurses tried to keep her calm. She told the press, "I had to be rushed to the hospital and have a thousand X-rays and I was totally in denial. I was screaming at the nurses; they weren't very happy with me. I just thought: 'Oh God, the rest of my summer's ruined, I won't be able to dance anymore, I won't be able to do yoga anymore. How long will I be an invalid and incapacitated?' I just freaked out." She also said the accident would not delay the release of her new album, *Confessions on a Dance Floor*, which was still on course to come out in November.

Right: Madonna in October 2005 at the première of *I'm Going To Tell You A Secret*, a documentary film covering the previous year's Re-Invention world tour. She introduced the movie herself, speaking about the difficulties she and director Jonas Akerlund had editing down all the hours of footage, which had proved a "traumatic experience." She added, "And like all traumatic experiences, we all ended up with more wisdom and less hair."

2006: Confessions Tour

Opposite and right: The Confessions tour began in Los Angeles in May, traveling around North America before going across to Britain and Europe and then on to Japan. It finished in Tokyo on September 21. The show had four sections: Equestrian, Bédouins, Glam-Punk Rock, and Disco and needed more than 400 costumes for Madonna and her dancers and musicians, most of which were designed by Jean-Paul Gaultier. The most controversial part of the show was when she performed "Live To Tell;" she appeared on a big mirrored crucifix wearing a crown of thorns. She sang the entire number "hanging" on the cross, as messages about AIDS, third-world poverty and grim statistics appeared above her on video screens. The reaction from some quarters was predictably one of outrage— The Evangelical Alliance said, "It is downright offensive. Madonna's use of Christian imagery is an abuse and it is dangerous." However, ABC News said, "Madonna is known for her theatrical, action-packed shows, and Sunday night's sold-out opener of her Confessions world tour was no exception." while the U.K. *Daily Star* decided, "The Disco Section was brilliant. She energetically did what she does best— danced her heart out complete with roller-skating dancers." As normal, tickets for all the shows sold out within minutes of going on sale at many of the venues.

Family rift...

Above: In June it was announced that Madonna had signed a contract with fashion giant H&M to supply a complete off stage wardrobe for her entire touring troupe including band, dancers, crew members, and the Material Girl herself. "Team Madonna" participants would choose clothing from H&M's extensive 2006 collection. The collaboration included a specially designed Madonna tracksuit, as well as an advertising campaign featuring Madonna and her dancers.

Opposite: In July 2006, *Life With my Sister Madonna*, written by younger brother Christopher, was published. The tell-all book was not authorized by Madonna and told unflattering stories of her behavior. It painted her husband, Guy Ritchie, in a particularly poor light, claiming the director's homophobia drove a wedge between the siblings. However, many reviewers noted that Christopher's lurid view of events didn't stop him going to his sister for help and financial support.

A new member of the family

Opposite: In October, controversy broke out when Madonna filed for adoption of a baby from a Malawian orphanage. She had been granted an interim order to adopt 13-month-old David Banda by the Malawian high court, after spending a week in the African country to assess projects she funded there, and David flew to London as soon as his passport and visa issues were resolved. A coalition of 67 rights groups quickly began a high court action to stop the adoption, alleging that the Malawi government had fast-tracked the process and broken its own laws by allowing the boy to be flown to London before the adoption process—which usually took 18 months—was finalized. They also claimed that the baby's father, Yohane Banda, had not understood that adoption meant giving up his son for ever and that he had since

withdrawn his permission. However, the father later appealed for an end to the legal challenge. Speaking on the eve of the hearing in Lilongwe, Malawi, Banda said, "I appeal to them to stop it because I don't want Madonna to get annoyed to the point of wanting to send back my David." Banda said local rights groups were "on my neck every day to support the court action... I am confused as to whose interests these human rights organizations are serving... Madonna is helping to take David out of poverty and possible death from diseases, and yet these people want to spoil everything." In an interview on U.S. talk show *Oprah*, Madonna insisted the adoption process was being conducted properly and she had not used her vast wealth to fast-track the process

Live Earth

Opposite and left: Madonna's performance was the finale of the Live Earth concert, which aimed to raise awareness and halt global warming. A review in U.K. newspaper The *Independent on Sunday* said, "For a symbolic moment, the 'non-essential' lights were turned off... Madonna stepped into a single spotlight, wearing a modest black dress that said she was being serious and sang, 'Hey you, don't give up.' There was even what looked like the choir of a posh private school, but the assembly mood didn't last as Madonna strapped on a metal-style electric guitar for 'Ray of Light': 'If you want to save the planet I want to see you jump up and down.' Nobody knows how to play a stadium like this woman and for the first time Wembley felt full. 'La Isla Bonita' was accompanied by manic gypsy punks Gogol Bordekki and morphed into the stomping finale 'Hung Up.' Rich rock stars telling us to change our lightbulbs had felt laughable all day, but for a moment Madonna made it seem like global warming could be stopped—with dancing."

Visiting Jerusalem

Opposite: Madonna with Israeli President Shimon Peres at the beginning of September. She had arrived in Israel on the eve of the Jewish new year to attend a conference on Kabbalah, and met Peres at his official Jerusalem residence. The two exchanged gifts, with Madonna receiving a lavishly bound copy of the Old Testament and Peres a volume of *The Book of Splendor*, the guiding text of Kabbalah.

Right: September was also the publication month of four books in a new series of *The English Roses*: *Friends For Life!*, *Goodbye Grace?*, *The New Girl* and *A Rose By Any Other Name*. The original *English Roses book*, released in 2003, had sold more than 500,000 copies internationally.

Meanwhile social workers were visiting Madonna at home in London, as a final step in the process of confirming her adoption of David Banda—which, as Liz Rosenberg, her spokesperson, pointed out, had followed all the correct legal steps and taken the normal 18 months. It looked clear that the adoption would be granted—and newspapers soon began to speculate that Madonna planned to adopt a second child, a little girl called Mercy.

Raising funds for Malawi

Left: Madonna with David Banda in New York. The family reportedly spoke to baby David in three languages: Madonna and her husband Guy Ritchie spoke to him in English, daughter Lourdes spoke to him in French and the whole family had classes in the Malawian tongue Chichewa. In December 2007, the star was finally given the approval to proceed with the adoption of David, and told the press that it was the best Christmas gift she had ever received. She was still apparently interested in finding him a sister, but the little girl Mercy—who she had reportedly hoped to adopt—still had close relatives who appeared reluctant to give permission.

Opposite: Madonna and Lourdes attending "A Night to Benefit Raising Malawi and UNICEF," which took place on February 6 in a purpose-built structure on the North Lawn at the United Nations in New York City. Hosted by Madonna and luxury brand Gucci, the evening was dedicated to raising funds and awareness for orphans and children made vulnerable by HIV/AIDS in Africa, where over 11 million of the 48 million orphans had lost one or both parents to AIDS. The event successfully raised a total of approximately $5.5 million from ticket sales and a live auction, which was split equally between the U.S. Fund for UNICEF and Madonna's charity Raising Malawi.

I Am Because We Are…

Opposite: Madonna and Guy Ritchie arriving at the Cannes Film Festival on May 21, 2008, for the screening of the documentary, *I Am Because We Are*. Written, produced and narrated by Madonna, the documentary detailed concern about the lives of thousands of children in Malawi who had been orphaned by or lost close relatives to HIV/AIDS. It also showed the work of Madonna's charity, Raising Malawi. The title of the film was based on an African belief that we are all connected, and that the individual cannot survive without the community. The film received highly positive reviews, with U.K. newspaper *The Times* saying, "This rich material makes for a completely absorbing film. Certain scenes, such as women and children literally dying of AIDS in front of the camera, drew gasps from the shocked audience in the screening room at Cannes. It's impossible to tear your eyes away from the screen. Not that the film portrays Malawian people as innocent victims of circumstances beyond their control. Rissman doesn't shy away from the culture of drinking, crime and violence that is prevalent in the country. Together, he and Madonna have made a shocking and incredibly moving film that is much more than an extended Comic Relief appeal."

Right: At the New York screening of *Filth and Wisdom*, the first feature film written and directed by Madonna. The movie received generally positive reviews, but only had a limited release.

Rock and Roll Hall of Fame...

Left: On March 10, 2008, Madonna was inducted into the Rock and Roll Hall of Fame—on the first year she was eligible, since inductees had to have had their first hit record at least 25 years previously. A few days later, on March 17 she released "4 Minutes," which gave Madonna her 37th hit in the *Billboard* Top 100, thus beating Elvis Presley's record.

Opposite: With Britney Spears during a performance in Los Angeles on the Sweet and Sticky tour, which began on August 23 in Cardiff, Wales. The tour covered 30 countries around the world and finished in Tel Aviv, Israel, on September 2, 2009. It was originally planned to cover Australia as well, but the crash of the Australian dollar as a result of the recession prevented this. As had become standard on Madonna spectacles, the show was divided into several sections—this time four: Pimp, Old School, Gypsy, and Rave. The tour broke many records: on the first leg it grossed $282 million, to make it the highest grossing tour by a solo artist— breaking the previous record of the Confessions tour. During the course of the tour Madonna performed to over 3.5 million fans, grossing a total of $408 million—making this the highest grossing tour ever by a female artist.

Sweet and Sticky

Opposite and right: Reviews from the Sweet and Sticky tour were very positive. *The Daily Mail* said, "Nobody does a big stadium show quite like Madonna. She might be pop's greatest female icon, but she does not rest on her laurels and this was a theatrical, two-hour blockbuster, featuring 16 dancers and a 12-piece band." In the opinion of *USA Today*, "Even the superstar's most cynical critics couldn't walk away from her two-hour extravaganza at the Izod Center on Saturday night without being thoroughly wowed. It was not only the spectacle of the concert, but the performer herself, as she reasserted her musical relevance and dominance in her 25th year in the spotlight. ... Madonna is not the world's most gifted singer or dancer or even musician, but she may be its greatest performer."

Unfortunately, Madonna's private life was not going so well. Over the past 12 months there had been persistent rumors in the press that her marriage to Guy Ritchie was on the rocks. By all accounts, Madonna had had enough of the constant arguing "about everything" with Guy and felt he was not spending enough time with their children, while Guy was tired of constantly living with her strict healthy regime and relentless exercise program. Some friends reportedly said the couple had been living virtually separate lives since the start of 2008 and had even divided their homes into his and hers quarters so they could avoid each other. In October, after many official denials, it was finally confirmed that the two would be divorcing.

A new daughter, a new man...

Opposite: Madonna in Portofino in August 2009 with her new daughter, Mercy, new man, Jesus Luz, and son David. In June 2009, after a long battle, Madonna had finally been given permission to adopt Chifundo "Mercy" James, the little Malawian girl she had first seen in an orphanage some years earlier. Mercy's grandmother had at first opposed the adoption, but had now decided she would soon be too old to continue to care for the child. Mercy was quickly flown to Britain to join her new family. Meanwhile, Madonna—now in the process of divorcing Guy Ritchie— had met Jesus Luz, a 22-year-old Brazilian model, on a photoshoot. She invited him to join her on tour and the two of them were soon seen out and about together.

Right: A visit to see the fabled rose red city of Petra in September, after the closing show on the Sweet and Sticky tour held in Tel Aviv. Madonna and her children were now based in New York City and she had recently purchased a $25 million Georgian-style townhouse in the Upper East Side. The 26-room property was reported to have 13 bedrooms and 14 bathrooms.

MTV Video Music Awards

Opposite and left: On September 13, Madonna opened the MTV Video Music Awards at Radio City Music Hall in New York City by talking about her experiences with Michael Jackson. Five days later she released her new album *Celebration*, a third collection of her greatest hits—which also included three new songs. The album debuted at the top of the charts in the United Kingdom, Italy, and Ireland, and in other nations it debuted within the top ten. The title track was released as the first single of the album and became Madonna's fortieth No. 1 song on *Billboard*'s dance chart.

On October 26, Madonna attended the breaking ground ceremony for the Raising Malawi Academy for Girls, a new boarding school to be built outside Lilongwe, Malawi; the school was her gift to the country to educate the women of Malawi to become future leaders. She was accompanied by her four children—Lourdes, 13, Rocco, 9, and her two adopted children, Malawian-born Mercy, 3, and David, 4. During her trip Madonna also met with President Bingu wa Mutharika and visited some of the orphanages her charity supports.

Chronology
and
Discography

CHRONOLOGY

1958

Aug 16 Madonna Louise Ciccone is born in Bay City, Michigan to French-Canadian Madonna Louise (née Fortin) and Italian-American Silvio Ciccone. They already have two boys, Martin and Anthony, and later go on to have three more: Paula, Christopher and Melanie.

1963

Dec 1   Madonna's mother dies of breast cancer. Not long afterwards her father remarries, but Madonna does not get on that well with her step-mother.

1977

End   After deciding to pursue a career as a dancer, Madonna leaves the University of Michigan where she has been studying dance and moves to New York City. She works with modern dance troupes, but has to supplement her income by working as a waitress at Dunkin' Donuts.

1977

While working as a dancer on tour with French artist Patrick Hernandez, Madonna meets musician Dan Gilroy.

Madonna joins the Breakfast Club—a pop group that also included Dan Gilroy—and performs at various times as a drummer or guitarist and later also sings lead vocals.

Sep   Filming of the low budget movie *A Certain Sacrifice*, in which Madonna appears as Bruna, a woman with three sex slaves. The completed film was not released but came out on video in 1985 to cash in on Madonna's growing fame, despite her attempts to block it.

1980

After leaving the Breakfast Club, Madonna forms her own band, Emmy, along with former

boyfriend Stephen Bray who she had first met at the University of Michigan.

1982

Oct 6   Sire Records, part of the Warner Bros Records Group, signs Madonna and releases her first single, "Everybody".

Fall   Madonna begins dating African-American artist Jean-Michel Basquiat, but in early 1983 they split because of his escalating drug abuse.

1983

John "Jellybean" Benitez becomes Madonna's new romantic partner after they are introduced by Stephen Bray.

Jul 27   Madonna's debut album, *Madonna*, is released.

1984

Nov 12   A second studio album, *Like a Virgin*, is released and becomes Madonna's first No.1 hit in the *Billboard* charts. It is later listed as one of the Definitive 200 Albums of All Time by the Rock and Roll Hall of Fame and the National Association of Recording Merchandisers.

1985

Jan 10–11 During shooting on the video for "Material Girl" in Hollywood, Madonna meets actor Sean Penn.

Feb 15   Release of the coming-of-age movie *Vision Quest*, which features a brief performance by Madonna as a bar room singer performing "Crazy For You" and "Gambler".

Mar 29   Première of *Desperately Seeking Susan*, a movie starring Rosanna Arquette and co-starring Madonna, which quickly came to be considered as a "Madonna" film even though she only appears in a supporting role.

Apr 10   Start of The Virgin Tour in Seattle, Madonna's debut trip round North America. It finishes on June 11 in New York City.

Aug 16   Madonna marries Sean Penn in a very public ceremony held in Malibu.

1986

Aug 29   Première of *Shanghai Surprise*, a movie starring Madonna and Sean Penn and produced by ex-Beatle George Harrison. Despite its pedigree, the film is panned by the critics and does not do well at the box office.

Aug   Madonna appears in her first theatre role, as Lorraine in a workshop production of *Goose and Tomtom*, written by David Rabe. The play also stars her husband, Sean Penn.

1987

Jun 14   Start of Who's That Girl World Tour in Osaka, Japan. It covers Japan, North America, Sweden, France, Italy, Germany, United Kingdom, The Netherlands and Spain, and finishes on September 6 in Florence, Italy.

Aug 7   Première of the movie *Who's That Girl*, in which Madonna stars as a recently paroled criminal determined to find the people who framed her.

Dec   Madonna and Sean Penn file divorce papers, but later withdraw them.

1988

Madonna appears on Broadway playing the secretary, Karen, in *Speed the Plow*, written by David Mamet.

Dec 31   Sean Penn and Madonna officially separate.

1989

Jan 7   Divorce papers for Madonna and Sean Penn are filed again.

Mar 21   Madonna's fourth studio album, *Like a Prayer*, is released and is hailed by *Rolling Stone* as being "as close to art as pop music gets..."

Nov 3   Première of the *Bloodhounds of Broadway* film, a comedy musical based on four short stories by Damon Runyon. Madonna has a small part as showgirl-with-a-heart-of-gold Hortense Hathaway.

While filming *Dick Tracy*, Madonna begins a relationship with co-star Warren Beatty.

Sep 14   The divorce of Madonna and Sean Penn is finalized.

1990

Apr 13   Start of Blonde Ambition World Tour in Tokyo. It covers Japan, North America, England, Germany, The Netherlands, France and Italy. It finishes on August 5 in Nice in the South of France.

Jun 15   Première of *Dick Tracy*, a film based on the adventures of the comic strip character. Madonna co-stars as Breathless Mahoney, a nightclub entertainer with a secret life.

Fall   Madonna's relationship with Warren Beatty comes to an end, and she begins dating both model Tony Ward and rapper Vanilla Ice.

1991

Spring   Madonna's relationships with Tony Ward and Vanilla Ice both end.

May 10   *Truth or Dare/In Bed With Madonna* is released, covering the Blonde Ambition tour and giving some insights into Madonna's private life.

1992

Madonna forms her own entertainment company, Maverick, to cover film production, record production, music and book publishing, as well as television and merchandising. It is a joint venture with Time Warner.

Oct 21   Publication of *Sex*, Madonna's first coffee table photography book, that went on to sell nearly 1.5 million copies in 6 months

Mar 30   Release of *Shadows and Fog*, a black and white film directed by Woody Allen. Madonna has a cameo role as a tightrope artiste.

Jul 1   Release of *A League of Their Own*, a film based on the founding of the women's professional baseball league in America, in which Madonna plays Mae Mordabito.

1993

Jan 15   First release of *Body of Evidence*, a movie starring Madonna and Willem Dafoe, which was universally hated by the critics.

Sep 25   Start of The Girlie Show World Tour in London. It covers the United Kingdom, France, Israel, Turkey, North America, Puerto Rico, Argentina, Brazil, Australia and Japan. It finishes on December 19 in Tokyo.

Nov 19   Release of *Dangerous Game*, the first film by Madonna's Maverick production company. Madonna starred as Sara Jennings and received good reviews from the critics for her performance.

1994

Aug 18   Publication of *The Girlie Show*, a photographic record of life backstage during the previous year's The Girlie Show World Tour.

Oct 25   Madonna's sixth studio album, *Bedtime Stories*, is released. After public controversy about her increasingly outrageous sexual exploits over the last few years, the album marks a change of direction as Madonna tones down her image to show a softer side.
After meeting fitness trainer Carlos Leon, Madonna becomes romantically involved with him.

1995

Oct 13   Release of *Blue in the Face*, a comedy film in which Madonna has a cameo role as a Singing Telegram.

Dec 25   Release of *Four Rooms*, an anthology film set in a hotel with four segments, each with a different director. Madonna appears in "The Honeymoon Suite", directed by Allison Anders.

1996

Mar 22   Release of *Girl 6*, a film directed by Spike Lee about an out-of-work actress who gets a job at a phone sex operation. Madonna has a cameo role as a boss who interviews the actress.

Oct 14   Madonna's first child, daughter Lourdes Maria Ciccone Leon, is born.

Dec 4   At the *Billboard* Music Awards ceremony in Las Vegas, Madonna is presented with a Lifetime Achievement Award.

Dec 5   Publication of *The Making of Evita*, the behind-the-scenes story of the movie with a foreword by Madonna.

Dec 14   Première of *Evita*, starring Madonna as Eva Péron, which was nominated for five Oscars and won Best Music, Original Song for "You Must Love Me", sung by Madonna. Madonna also won a Golden Globe Award for Best Actress in a Musical.

1998

Oct   Publication of an audio CD, *The Emperor's New Clothes*, which features many celebrities including Madonna as the voice of the Empress.

Sting and his wife Trudie Styler introduce Madonna to British director Guy Ritchie.

1999

Feb 24   At the 41st Grammy Awards Madonna wins three awards for *Ray of Light*, including Best Dance Recording and Best Pop Album.

Sep 9   The MTV Video Music Award ceremony features a tribute to Madonna as the most nominated artiste in VMA history, with a series of drag performers each impersonating the singer in one of her music videos.

2000

Mar 3   Release of *The Next Best Thing*, the last film directed by John Schlesinger, which stars Madonna and Rupert Everett.

Aug 11   Madonna and Guy Ritchie's first son, Rocco, is born.

Dec 22   Skibo Castle in Scotland is the venue for the marriage of Madonna and Guy Ritchie.

2001

Jun 9   Start of Drowned World Tour in Barcelona. It covers Spain, Italy, Germany, France, England, and North America, finishing on Septr 15 in Los Angeles. It is one of the highest grossing concerts of the year, with most venues sold out.

2002

Oct 11   Release of *Swept Away*, a comedy drama directed by Guy Ritchie and starring Madonna.

Nov 18   Royal World Première of the Bond film *Die Another Day*, in which Madonna has a cameo role as a fencing instructor. She also releases the title song, which is nominated for a Golden Globe Award for Best Original Song.

Madonna makes her West End theatre debut in London, playing art dealer Loren in *Up For Grabs*, written by David Williamson.

2003

Publication of *X-STaTIC Pro=CeSS*, a limited edition photographic coffee table book, which accompanied an exhibition installation that Madonna has collaborated on with fashion photographer Steven Klein.

Aug 28   Madonna performs "Hollywood" at the MTV Awards with Britney Spears, Christina Aguilera and Missy Elliott. At one point she kisses Britney Spears and Christina Aguilera, which causes the Press to go wild.

Sep 15   *The English Roses*, a children's book by Madonna, receives the most widespread launch in publishing history when it is released in over 100 countries on the same day. It debuts at No. 1 on the *New York Times* Best Seller list.

Nov 10   Publication of *Mr Peabody's Apples*, a second children's book by Madonna, which also debuts at No. 1 on the *New York Times* Best Seller list.

2004

Jan   Release of *Nobody Knows Me*, a book of rare and unseen shots of Madonna's life, available only via digital download for one month from Madonna's official website.

Mar   Maverick sues Warner Music Group/Time Warner, alleging that their bad management and poor business practice has caused losses running into millions. Warner counter sues, alleging that Maverick is responsible for the loss. The dispute is resolved by Warner purchasing Madonna's shares in Maverick, but this does not release her from her recording contract with Warner.

Apr 26   Publication of *Yakov and the Seven Thieves*, Madonna's third children's book, which debuts at No. 7 on the *New York Times* Best Seller list.

May 24   Start of Re-Invention World Tour in Los Angeles. It Covers North America, England, Ireland, France, The Netherlands, and Portugal. It finishes in Lisbon, Portugal, on September 14.

Nov 11   Publication of *The Adventures of Abdi*, Madonna's fourth children's book, which reaches the Top Ten in the *New York Times* Best Seller list.

2005

Jan   Madonna performs John Lennon's "Imagine" during a Tsunami Aid concert.

Jun 2   Publication of *Lotsa Da Casha*, Madonna's fifth children's book, which reaches the Top Ten in the *New York Times* Best Seller list.

Jul 2   Madonna appears live at the Live 8 benefit concert.

Oct 21 MTV première of *I'm Going to Tell You a Secret*, a documentary film covering Madonna's 2004 Re-Invention World Tour.

2006

May 21 Start of Confessions Tour in Los Angeles. It covers North America, Wales, England, Italy, Germany, Denmark, France, The Netherlands, Czech Republic, Russia, and Japan. It finishes on September 21 in Tokyo.

Jul Publication of *Life With my Sister Madonna*, written by younger brother Christopher. The book is not authorized by Madonna and causes a family rift.

Mid year Fashion range H&M signs Madonna to become the worldwide face of its clothing range.

Oct 6 Publication of a boxed set of the five children's books and also release of an audio tape, *The English Roses and Other Stories*, featuring Madonna reading the stories herself.

Oct 10 Madonna files adoption papers for a Malawian boy, David Banda Mwale, whom she met when raising funds for the orphanage in which he lived.

Oct 24 Publication of *The English Roses: Too Good To Be True*, the sequel to Madonna's best selling first children's book.

Dec 13 First general release of *Arthur and the Invisibles (Arthur and the Minimoys* in non-English speaking countries), a part live-action and part-animated film in which Madonna is the voice of Princess Selenia.

2007

Madonna launches her fashion line, M by Madonna, worldwide.

Jul At the London Live Earth concert, Madonna performs her new single, "Hey You".

Sep 13 Publication of *The English Roses: Friends For Life!*, *The English Roses: Goodbye Grace?*, *The English Roses: The New Girl* and *The English Roses: A Rose By Any Other Name*, the first four books in a new series of *The English Roses* stories.

Oct Madonna announces her departure from Warner Bros. Records since she has signed a new ten-year contract with Live Nation, which is worth $120 million.

2008

Mar 10 Madonna is inducted into the Rock and Roll Hall of Fame

Mar 17 Release of "4 Minutes", which gives Madonna her 37th hit in the Billboard Top 100, beating Elvis Presley's record.

Apr 24 First release of *I Am Because We Are*, a documentary about the orphans of Malawi, that was written, produced and narrated by Madonna.

May 28 The adoption of David Banda Mwali is finalized and he is renamed David Banda Mwali Ciccone Ritchie.

May 29 Publication of *The English Roses: Big Sister Blues*, the fifth book in the new series of *The English Roses* stories.

Jul 17 Publication of *The English Roses: Being Binah*, the sixth book in the new series of *The English Roses* stories.

Aug 23 Start of Sweet & Sticky Tour in Cardiff, Wales. It covers Wales, France, Germany, Switzerland, The Netherlands, Germany, England, Portugal, Spain, France, Austria, Montenegro, Greece. North America, Argentina, Chile, Brazil, Belgium, Italy, Norway, Russia, Estonia, Scandinavia, Czech Republic, Poland, Hungary, Serbia, Romania, and Bulgaria, and finishes in Tel Aviv, Israel, on Sep 2, 2009.

Sep 11 Publication of *The English Roses: Hooray For The Holidays*, the seventh book in the new series of *The English Roses* stories.

Sep 17 Release of *Filth and Wisdom*, the first film directed by Madonna. It received generally favourable reviews.

Oct 1 Publication of *Madonna Confessions*, a photography book documenting the 2006 Confessions Tour.

Oct Madonna files for divorce from husband Guy Ritchie.

Oct After meeting Jesus Luz, a 22-year-old Brazilian model, on a photoshoot Madonna invites him on tour with her and the two of them are soon seen out and about together.

Dec 26 Publication of *The English Roses: A Perfect Pair*, the eighth book in the new series of *The English Roses* stories.

2009

Jan 8 Publication of *I Am Because We Are*, a book with photographs and excerpts from interviews with Malawian children, based on the documentary of the same name. The book features a foreword by Madonna.

Mar 2 The Recording Industry Association of Japan awards Madonna the Japan Gold International Artist of the Year.

Jun 12 The Supreme Court of Malawi grants Madonna the right to adopt Chifundo Mercy James.
Sep 13 At the MTV Music Awards, Madonna appears to pay tribute to Michael Jackson.

Oct 26 Madonna attends the breaking ground ceremony for the Raising Malawi Academy for Girls, a new boarding school to be built outside Lilongwe, Malawi. The school is her gift to the country to educate the women of Malawi to become future leaders.

Nov 12 Publication of *Madonna: Sticky & Sweet*, a photography book documenting the Sticky & Sweet Tour.

2010

Jan 7 Publication of *The English Roses: Runway Rose*, the ninth book in the new series of *The English Roses* stories.

DISCOGRAPHY
ALBUMS

1983
Jul 27   *Madonna*

1984
Nov 12   *Like a Virgin*

1986
Jun 30   *True Blue*

1987
Jul 21   *Who's That Girl* (soundtrack album)
Nov 17   *You Can Dance* (compilation album)

1989
Mar 21   *Like a Prayer*

1990
May 22   *I'm Breathless* (soundtrack album)
Nov 9   *The Immaculate Conception* (compilation album)

1992
20 Oct   *Erotica*

1994
Oct 25   *Bedtime Stories*

1995
Nov 7   *Something to Remember* (compilation album)

1996
Oct 25   *Evita* (soundtrack album)

1998
Mar 3   *Ray of Light*

2000
Sep 19   *Music*

2001
Nov 13   *GHV2* (compilation album)

2003
Apr 23   *American Life*
Nov 24   *Remixed & Revisited* (compilation album)

2005
Nov 15   *Confessions on a Dance Floor*

2006
Jun 20   *I'm Going to Tell You a Secret* (live album)

2007
Jan 30   *The Confessions Tour* (live album)

2008
Apr 29   *Hard Candy*

2009
Sept 18   *Celebration* (compilation album)

SINGLES

1982
Oct 6   "Everybody"/"Everybody"

1983
Mar 9   "Burning up"/"Physical Attraction"

Sep 7   "Holiday"/"I Know It" (UK B side "Think of Me")

1984
Feb 15   "Borderline"/"Think Of Me"

Apr 19   "Lucky Star"/"I Know It"

Nov 6   "Like a Virgin"/"Stay"

1985
Jan 30   "Material Girl"/"Pretender"

Mar 2   "Crazy For You"/"Gambler"

Ap 10   "Angel"/"Into the Groove" (UK B side "Burning Up")

Jul 23   "Into the Groove"/"Shoo-Bee-Do" (in UK, released August 10th in Japan with "Physical Attraction" as B side)

Jul 24   "Dress You Up"/"Shoo-Bee-Do" (UK B side "I Know It")

Oct 3   "Gambler"/"Nature of the Beach" (Europe only, October 21 in Japan)

1986
Mar 26   "Live To Tell"/"Live To Tell" (instrumental) (released UK April 21)
Jun 11   "Papa Don't Preach"/"Pretender"/"Ain't No Big Deal"

Sep 29   "True Blue"/"Holiday" (UK only, October 9 in US with "Ain't No Big Deal" on B side)

Nov 12   "Open Your Heart"/"White Heat" (Europe B side "Lucky Star)

1987
Feb 25   "La Isla Bonita"/"La Isla Bonita" (instrumental) (UK release March 31)

Jun 30   "Who's That Girl"/"White Heat" (released July 14 in UK)

Aug 25   "Causing A Commotion"/"Jimmy, Jimmy" (released Sept 15 in UK, October 10 Japan)

Nov 25   "The Look Of Love"/"I Know It"

1988
Apr 25   "Spotlight"/"Where's The Party" (only released in Japan)

1989
Feb 28   "Like A Prayer"/"Act of Contrition" (released March 6 in UK, March 16 Japan)

May 9   "Express Yourself"/"The Look of Love"

Aug 1   "Cherish"/"Supernatural"

Oct 24   "Oh Father"/"Pray for Spanish Eyes"

Dec 10   "Dear Jessie"/"Till Death Do Us Part"

1990

Jan 30   "Keep It Together"/"Keep It Together" (instrumental) only released in US and on March 25 in Japan.

Mar 20   "Vogue"/"Keep It Together" ("Vogue: Betty Davis Dub" in US)

Jun 30   "Hanky Panky"/"More" (released July 15 in UK)

Nov 6   "Justify My Love"/"Express Yourself" (released December 2 in UK and December 10 in Japan)

1991

Feb 26   "Rescue Me"/"Rescue Me" (UK release April 7, B side "Spotlight")

1992

Jun 16   "This Used To Be My Playground"/"This Used To Be My Playground" (released July 19 in UK, July 25 in Japan)

Oct 11   "Erotica"/"Erotica" (instrumental) (UK only, released US October 13)

Dec 6   "Deeper and Deeper"/"Deeper and Deeper" (UK release only, US December 8)

1993

Feb 22   "Bad Girl"/"Fever" (US and Japan, European B side "Erotica")

Mar 22   "Fever"/"Fever"

Jul 17   "Rain"/"Waiting"/"Up Down Suite" (UK B side "Open Your Heart", released July 25)

Nov 7   "Bye Bye Baby"/"Rain" (released November 28, Japan)

1994

Mar 8   "I'll Remember"/"Secret Garden"

Sep 28   "Secret"/"Secret" (UK B side "Let Down Your Guard", released October 2)

Dec 6   "Take a Bow"/"Take a Bow" (January 21, 1995 in UK)

1995

Feb 13   "Bedtime Story"/"Survival" (released April 11 in US)

Jun 6   "Human Nature"/"Sanctuary" (released August 20 in UK and Europe, B side in Japan "La Isla Bonita")

Oct 28   "You'll See"/"Live To Tell" (B side in Europe and Japan, "Rain")

1996

Mar 17   "One More Chance"/"Verás"

Mar 10   "Love Don't Live Here Anymore"/"Over and Over" (Japan only)

Oct 27   "You Must Love Me"/"Rainbow High" (US October 28)

Feb 4   "Don't Cry For Me Argentina"/"Don't Cry For Me Argentina"

1997

Mar 24   "Another Suitcase In Another Hall"/"Don't Cry For Me Argentina" (UK only)

1998

Feb 23   "Frozen"/"Shanti"/"Ashtangi"

May 6   "Ray of Light"/"Has To Be" (US May 11)

Aug 24   "Drowned World"/"Substitute for Love"/"Sky Fits Heaven"

Sep 22   "The Power of Good-Bye"/"Mer Girl"/"Little Star" (Europe November 16, Japan November 26)

1999

Mar 2   "Nothing Really Matters"/"To Have and Not To Hold" (US April 13, Japan April 21)

Jun 1   "Beautiful Stranger"

2000

Mar 3   "American Pie"/"American Pie"

Aug 29   "Music"/"Cyberraga"

Nov 21   "Don't Tell Me"/"Cyberraga" (US release January 16, 2001 with "Don't Tell Me" as B side)

2001

Apr 17   "What it Feels Like for a Girl"/"Lo Que Siente La Mujer"

2002

Oct 22   "Die Another Day"/"Die Another Day"

2003

Apr 8   "American Life"/"Die Another Day" (US, but available as digital download from March 24. Released April 14 in Europe)

Jul 3   "Hollywood"/"Hollywood" (Europe, July 8 US)

Oct 20   "Me Against the Music" (with Britney Spears)

Nov 21   "Nothing Fails"/"Nobody Knows Me" (Europe B side "Love Profusion")

Dec 8   "Love Profusion"/"Nobody Knows Me" (Europe and Australia only

2004

Mar 16   "Love Profusion"/"Nothing Fails" (North America and Europe only)

2005

Oct 17   "Hung Up"/"Hung Up"

2006

Feb 28   "Sorry"/"Let It Will Be"

Jun 6   "Get Together"/"I Love New York"

Oct 31   "Jump"/"History"

2007

May 16   "Hey You" (free digital download for 7 days in aid of charity, paid download from May 24)

2008

Mar 17   "4 Minutes"/"4 Minutes" (featuring Justin Timberlake)

Jun 4   "Give it 2 Me" (digital download and cd)

Oct 17   "Miles Away" (digital download and cd)

2009

Jul 31   "Celebration" (digital download and cd)

The publishers would like to thank Getty Images for their help in providing the images used in this book. Particular thanks to Hayley Newman and Martina Oliver.

Thanks also to Kate Truman and Melanie Cox for their help in producing the book.